"In *A Life Worth Waiting For!*, Dwight Lee Wolter verbally powerfully describes growing up in a dysfunctional family. More significantly, he shares the processes, feelings, and rewards of recovery. His story is a moving book that touches the deep pain—and the possible joy—shared by adult children of alcoholics."

> Sharon Wegscheider-Cruse, lecturer;
> president, Onsite Training and Consulting;
> founding board chairperson, National Association
> for Children of Alcoholics (NACoA);
> author, *Another Chance* and *Choicemaking*.

"This material was extremely moving. It made me laugh and then cry.... I enthusiastically endorse his work."

> John Bradshaw, author,
> *Bradshaw On: The Family* and
> *Healing the Shame that Binds You*

"Heart-rending, almost painfully eloquent in its honesty, Dwight Lee Wolter's *A Life Worth Waiting For!* is a triumph of the human spirit. Pick up the best novel you can find, and read this book instead!"

> F. Forrester Church, Ph.D., minister,
> Unitarian Church of All Souls, New York;
> Chicago Tribune columnist;
> author of *Everyday Miracles: Stories from Life*

"A special and unusual book that tells a painful and all too common story in a sensitive and honest way. I shared it with my children and it stimulated some very meaningful dialogue within our family. I hope it will enjoy the acceptance and visibility it deserves as it illuminated another corner of what Bob Ackerman describes as 'living in the shadow.'"

    H. Stephen Glenn, president,
    Sunrise Associates

"A courageous and intimate look at the impact of alcohol across generations. Dwight Lee Wolter's clear understanding and compassion for his own inner child has helped us to realize that we, too, can break the cycle of addiction with our own children."

    Patricia A. O'Gorman, Ph.D.,
    co-author, *Breaking the Cycle of Addiction*

"Deeply moving and compelling. The candor is startling and impressive.... I can't imagine anyone not identifying with the feelings Dwight Lee Wolter so adroitly displays and the hope his message delivers."

    Kenneth Waissman, Tony-Award winning
    Broadway producer: *Grease, Agnes of God,*
    Torch Song Trilogy, and *The Days of Wine and Roses*

A LIFE WORTH WAITING FOR!

Dwight Lee Wolter

CompCare® Publishers
Minneapolis, Minnesota

©1989 by Dwight Lee Wolter
All rights reserved.
Published in the United States
by CompCare Publishers.

Reproduction in whole or part, in any form, including storage in memory device system, is forbidden without written permission... except that portions may be used in broadcast or printed commentary or review when attributed fully to author and publication by names.

Library of Congress Cataloging-in-Publication Data

Wolter, Dwight Lee.
    A life worth waiting for/Dwight Lee Wolter.
        P.   cm.
    ISBN 0-89638-150-1 :
    1. Wolter, Dwight Lee. 2. Adult children of alcoholics—United States—Biography. 3. Adult children of alcoholics—United States—Poetry. I. Title.
HV5132.W65 1988
362.2'92—dc19
[B]

Cover design by Jeremy Gale
Cover photo by Al Mauro

Interior design by MacLean and Tuminelly
Cut-paper illustrations by Nancy Tuminelly,
adapted from Dwight Lee Wolter's original art

"Hyde Park" was previously published in *Belly Lint*, Quest Publishing.
"Hotel' was previously published in *Blueprints*, Nobody Press.
"Parenting Myself and My Daughter" was published in *Changes* magazine.

Inquiries, orders, and catalog requests should be addressed to
CompCare Publishers
2415 Annapolis Lane
Minneapolis, MN 55441
Call toll free 800/328-3330
(Minnesota residents 612/559-4800)

5   4   3   2   1
93 92 91 90 89

This book is dedicated to my friend and teacher
Stewart Freeman

Names and identities of people mentioned in this book
have been changed to protect the guilty
as well as an occasional innocent

PART ONE
GROWING UP CRAZY
My relationship with my parents

1

PART TWO
FRIENDS, LOVERS, AND OTHER STRANGERS
How my childhood has affected my adult relationships

41

PART THREE
TO PARENT
How my upbringing in a crazy family has helped and hindered my parenting of my daughter—and myself

95

PART FOUR
I SMELL FREEDOM
Hope for and belief in recovery and in myself

159

How does someone who has grown up with alcoholism or abuse find a new life, free of past ghosts and present insecurities? By reaching in and reaching out. By seeing through the gloss of denial to what *really* happened, facing it, and then releasing it. By moving past numbness, sadness, and anger, to a vantage of understanding—perhaps even forgiveness.

Here is one man's supercharged, highly personal proclamation of freedom voiced in a collection of thoughts, memories, and insights. Here in Dwight Lee Wolter's vivid verbal snapshots, are candids Adult Children of Alcoholics may see in their own family albums—of childhoods haunted by secrets, isolation, sabotaged self-esteem, emotional chaos, spiritual poverty. But here, too, emerging from the process of healing, are hope and humor and openness and recovery.

Startlingly honest, ultimately triumphant, this is much more than a book—it's a life-changing experience.

Holding myself at bay
like a scientist
huddled over a microscope
peering at creation,
I methodically glued
some of my words together
and got this...

PART ONE

GROWING UP CRAZY

GROWING UP CRAZY

I performed a magic trick when I was a child. I made my Self disappear. I hid behind people. I became part of the furniture. I soaked into the carpet like a spilled drink. Every day was a challenge to find new ways to became invisible. I believed that if my parents couldn't see me, then they couldn't hurt me. Like an ostrich I buried my head in the sand and assumed myself invisible. I buried my feelings, my desires, and my love deep within the earth where no one could find them. Including me.

One day, as an adult, I decided I had had enough of life without feelings. I went digging for my Self. I found nothing. Like a fearful dog who buries a bone and then runs hungrily around the yard because he can't remember where he hid it, I excavated all the ruins of my life looking for a Self, only to discover that there was no Self to be found. Had I decayed like bits of a picnic buried at the beach? By hiding my Self from my parents I hid my Self from me. The pathetic part of this story is that this hiding of my Self had not spared me from the ravages of life with my parents. They took their self-hatred out on their children. A target in the dark is still a target. And like a heat-seeking missile, their abuse found me no matter where I hid.

Today I am putting together the puzzle I call myself. I am missing some of the pieces. One big missing piece is called my youth. I am traveling backward to recover the little boy I call my Self, so that I can resolve some of the issues presented in this book and get on with what is left of my adult life. I am, in essence, going through adolescence at thirty-five. Better late than never.

The pages of this book are like snapshots. There are two invisible people in each photo. One is the Self I had to bury because I couldn't stand the pain of my childhood. The other is the Self I want to become.

I have to coax them into visibility. This book is the developing fluid I soak the snapshots in, so a clear picture can be made from the negative. This book, this verbal photo album, illustrates the process of the recovery of my life from the rubble of my past.

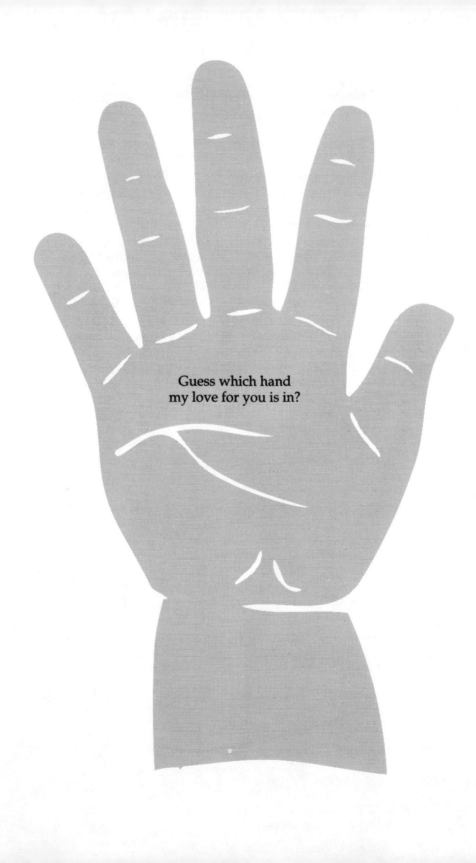

KEEP 'EM GUESSING

My mother made two fists behind her back
then brought them both around to the front
and said "Guess which hand my love for you
is in?"

After playing this game several times
and never guessing the correct hand I said
"Hey! Wait a minute! Open both hands at the
same time."

She did and I bet you aren't surprised
but I sure as hell was to discover
that both of her hands were empty.

Just because someone is withholding
something from you doesn't mean
they have it to offer.

I LEARN MY LESSONS WELL

Different families teach different things. Some families teach love and understanding. Some families teach the value of hard work. My family taught insanity and hatred.

I learned how to hate from a wonderful, loving, caring, drunken mother. She taught me how to hate my father. She taught me that every time something bad happened to my father it was God punishing him for the way he treated her. She taught me that God was on her side. She told me that Satan was on my father's side. She taught me how to focus all my hatred and fear and sense of abandonment on my father, so that I wouldn't see how much she too was a drunk who neglected me as much as my father did. Dealing with my father was painful, but easy. It was not hard to pin the tail on that donkey. He was a violent drunk. A wife-beater and child-abuser. But my mother skillfully wrapped her neglect in the guise of love. She taught me how to hate everything but her.

I learned how to be insane from my father. Being insane was the only thing he ever mastered. It was all he had to offer. He taught me to fear. He taught me to fear everything I cannot see, including germs and God. So that is what I learned. He taught me that the world is an unsafe place populated by people who can't be trusted. He taught me to anticipate people's thoughts so that I could plan my reaction to them.

He taught me to trust no one. He taught me to be a target. He taught me never to ask for what I wanted. He taught me to not need. He taught me to live on clues. He taught me to distrust comfort. He taught me that friendship was functionless. He taught me that honesty would be used against me. He taught me that love was inconvenient. He taught me to not accept kindness from others because of the indebtedness it creates. He taught me to prepare myself for nothing because nothing would come true. He taught me numbness. He taught me to fear change. He taught me to detonate calmness. He taught me that the human body is a temple of filth. He taught me paranoia. He taught me to treat myself like a hostile stranger.

These lessons helped me to survive my childhood. My home was governed by insane rules and beliefs. And insane rules call for insane behavior. Today my life has changed for the better and insanity as a way of life is no longer needed or appropriate. I must learn new everything. I am a warehouse packed with outmoded goods which I am in the process of unloading. The sifting and carting seem to take forever. But I am enjoying the process of creating space to be filled with healthy and exciting things I need and deserve. I am well on my way to a life worth living.

FAMILY

I cry for the loss of what I never had.
I yearn for a glimpse of sights
I have never seen.
I treasure the memory of love I only
imagined to be.
I must give up hoping against hope
for a better yesterday.

Here are thirty-five years of tears coming out
in one hour. I have to roll up my pant
cuffs to wade through them.
Here are the tears for all the years
I thought I was alive.
I grieve the loss of the child I never was.
I have spent my life pretending
the first half of my life never happened.
I refuse to face you or me or the truth
about you or me.
I mourn the loss of the boy I never knew.
To have lived all one's life without a trace
of the sense of family or home
means you can't really be human, can you?
Well, can you?
I fear the answer.

MY FATHER USED TO MAKE ME WAIT

My father made me wait in the car outside a bar while he was pickling his head in a jar of gin. I wouldn't go in. The sun was blazing hot. The apple on the dashboard began to rot. Hours later he moved the car into the shade and offered me a lemonade. I listened to the car radio so long that the battery was almost dead. The Top 40 songs were spinning in my head. They were songs of love and devotion. "Come on, baby, do the Locomotion."

Finally I couldn't take the heat, so I sauntered into the bar, head down, reeking of defeat. I felt I had to join the enemy in order to survive. My father smiled as his child bellied-up to the bar. "Just like a little man," his wobbly eyes said to me as he placed a coke in my hand.

Then he would treat me to a game of eight-ball, but he was so wasted the cue kept falling out of his hand. That was the game to play every Saturday. Hit the balls into the bottomless pockets and they disappeared into thin air as if they were never there. When the table is bare you win. Then you order a drink and start all over again. All over again. Over again. And again.

If you say you are famished, Daddy will buy you a sandwich. I was raised on barfood. Barffood.

Finally, oh finally, Daddy says, "We've had enough fun, son. We gotta run." Driving home on the westside highway, Daddy's ears begin to ring. "Sing! Sing to me! Sing to me, son. I'm beginning to fall asleep at the wheel. It must be this August heat. So unless you want our bodies strewn across the street you had better sing to me." So I sang the only two songs I knew that he liked (Mommy taught them to me when I was three): "Don't Fence Me In" and "You Always Hurt the One You Love."

And so, la-dee-da, life goes on and on and on. And by the age of twelve I lived in hell every Saturday, which was my day to be with Daddy when he would belly-up to the bar and I would wait in the car. And wait in the car. And wait. But we always tried to make it home before too late at night so that we could turn on the television and watch the Saturday night fight.

THE WAY A CHILD OF AN ALCOHOLIC IS TAUGHT THE DAYS OF THE WEEK

Today is Friday.
Tomorrow is not.
Yesterday wasn't either.
Day after tomorrow
is pretty close.

The day after that is very far away.
One more day from then
and you've rounded the bend
and are close to today again.
The day after that
and you're over the hump.
The day after that
is yesterday again.
And that brings us back to Friday.

Now, sweetheart,
it is your turn
to recite the days
of the week.
What do you mean you don't know?
I just taught you.

GOOD GRADES

I showed my report card to my father.
"You got all V's! What the hell
is the matter with you?" he asked.
I took the report card out of his
drunken hand, turned it upside down,
and handed it back to him.
"Ahhh. You got all A's. That's what
I expected of you," he said to me
and continued watching championship
wrestling on our black–and–white
television.

THE FOOD IS SLOWLY BURNING

The food is slowly burning
in the oven.
I want to eat.
It is eleven at night.
Daddy ain't coming home.
He ain't hungry for you
or your burnt food, Mommy.
Feed me!
I have to go to school tomorrow.
What did I do wrong?
Why do I have to wait?

I am thirty-five now.
I am still waiting
for Mommy to feed me burnt food.
You don't have to tell me
the food ain't coming.
I ain't stupid.
Tell the kid inside me
that the food ain't coming.
He is the one doing all the waiting.
He is the one
twiddling his thumbs
while he is learning how to hate.
Daddy he can understand.
Daddy is a drunk.
That one is easy.
Daddy acts like a drunk.
But what about Mommy?
Daddy is at the bar
so her son don't get to eat?
What did I do wrong?
Why do I have to wait?

GOLDFISH

When I was a kid I went to a neighborhood fair and played a game. The object of the game was to stand behind a white line several yards away from a bunch of very small goldfish bowls and try to throw a Ping-Pong ball into one of them. If the ball went into the bowl you won the goldfish. The mouth of the bowl was very small, not much larger than the Ping-Pong balls, and it was not easy to win the game.

The amount of money I spent by far surpassed the value of the goldfish, but I continued to play until even the game operator was rooting for me to win. I kept throwing the balls as if I were in a trance, not looking where they were going. I was staring at the poor goldfish. The bowls were so small the fish could barely turn around in them, let alone swim. I knew what it was like to feel trapped and unable to move in your own home. My mission was to liberate the fish from the suffering I knew so well.

I finally won. The man dumped the goldfish and the water into a plastic bag and tied a knot at the opening. "Ya bitter git dis fish 'ome quik afore da ting dies," he said to me. I walked as fast as I could without running because I figured the fish was upset enough as it was without being bounced around.

When I got home I walked past my father who was passed out in front of the television. I went into the kitchen and tried to show my mother what I had won, but she was busy doing something. She was always doing something. She always seemed very far away, as if she were thinking secret thoughts of much greater importance than a child with a goldfish.

I reached into the cupboard and got out a large glass salad bowl and put it in the sink under the faucet. I turned on the cold water and filled the bowl. I scooped the goldfish out of the plastic bag and said to him, "You're free now! You have a new, large, beautiful home. I'm going to buy some pretty rocks to put in the bottom of it. Now you can swim!" I put the goldfish into the bowl and as soon as it touched the water it stiffened, turned belly up, and died.

I reached into the bowl to pick up the fish and scalded my hand. I shrieked! My mother turned to see what I was doing. Through tears and gestures and sobby words I communicated the story to her. She explained to me that she had just finished doing the dishes and there must have been a lot of hot water still in the faucet even though I had turned on the cold water. She comforted me for a moment and then ground up the goldfish in the garbage disposal. "You should ask me before you do these things, Dwight," she said in a soft tone as she washed the salad bowl and placed it back in the cupboard.

JELLY-FILLED DOUGHNUTS

My first drug of choice was jelly-filled doughnuts. We found a bakery that would deliver them every morning. The delivery man liked me and we developed a minor friendship. Sometimes he would give me free day-old doughnuts.

But soon the sickness in my family began to fester so badly that we oozed a puddle of poison under our door and the delivery man couldn't help but notice it. I saw his face begin to change. His smile became tighter. He stared straight ahead, as if he were afraid to look into the panic in a child's eyes, as if he were afraid to let his eyes wander around the room because of what he might see. Occasionally he must have heard the 6:30 A.M. screaming. He must have seen me performing my forced trek of carrying huge bags full of empty quarts of beer to the garbage before the neighbors woke up. He must have seen my mother's battered face, or the children walking around bumping into each other, haggard from another sleepless night of listening to the rage and violence. The delivery man began to withdraw from me. I understood. It must have been very painful to have a friendship with an abused child.

The time came when we could no longer pay the bill for the jelly-filled doughnuts. The delivery man must have been relieved not to have to come to our house anymore. But I never got to say good-bye. I hope we didn't stick him with the bill. I missed seeing his clean-shaven face, his starched white shirt, his shined shoes, his well-rested eyes. He was my daily, morning reminder that life existed outside of our house. He showed me that there were normal people in the world who did beautiful, mundane things. When he left, my hope left with him. I didn't know it at the time, at least not on a conscious level, but I probably wished that he would be the person who would see what was going on in the nuthouse I lived in and somehow get me out of there. But it just didn't happen and I gave up hoping for salvation. I got a dizzy sensation and I felt that I was swirling downward like water in a toilet bowl. Into the hidden pipes. Between the walls. Of madness.

HE KNOCKED AND THE DISEASE ANSWERED

I threw a snowball at a truck. The driver, I discovered, was quite athletic. He stopped the truck, turned off the engine, ran after me, and caught me less than a block away. He got me by the back of my neck and marched me to my parents' house. "We'll see what your father has to say about this, you little punk," he snorted.

My father opened the door. He was drunk, unshaven, beet-red. He had the look in his eye of a wounded wolf backed into a corner. His eyes were glassy and narrow. He was territorial, crouched, and ready to spring. If there was anything my father hated it was a stranger, and everyone was a stranger to him. My mother was crying and pacing in the background. The air was pungent with the smell of pork and beer and sauerkraut and cigarettes.

"Your son here threw a snowball at my truck," the man said in a meek, thin voice. It was as if he was telling Hitler that one of his generals had said a naughty word.

"Oh, yeah?" my father said, unimpressed. "You shouldn't do that," my father added in a monotone.

I could tell the truck driver just wanted this thing over with. He wanted out, quickly. I began to enjoy his discomfort. It was my vicarious revenge. I probably could have got him to apologize for his truck being in the way of my snowball.

My father looked intently at the driver's hand that was still on the back of my neck. The driver slowly pulled it away, said good-bye, turned, and walked quickly down the street. I walked up the street, in the opposite direction. My father closed the door. We all went about our business.

GUILT-ASSUMER

My father had my mother committed to the psychiatric unit of a private hospital. He told the staff that her problem was that she was insane. The fact is that she was alcoholic. They put her in a room without giving her any medication and she went into withdrawal, had a cerebral hemorrhage, and has been paralyzed ever since.

I was away at a speech competition when it happened. I received notice from my coach that I had to return home immediately after the competition, which was about to begin. I won the state championship in original oratory that day. I have always suspected that the judge's pity for me secured my victory.

When I got home my father told me that my mother had been worried sick about me being away from home for the first time. He reminded me that I hadn't called. He said that if I hadn't been away from home, and if I hadn't been such a pain in the ass, then this wouldn't have happened to my mother. I dismissed his ranting as insanity. But, although I was not thoroughly convinced, I suspected it could be true.

My father insinuated that if I had only stayed small and passive and insignificant, if only I hadn't tried to reach for recognition from people outside the family, if only I hadn't grown up and begun taking positive actions on my behalf, if only I hadn't attempted to break away from the symbiotic relationship I had with my mother—then this would not have happened to her.

I believed that alcoholic nonsense for quite a while until I realized my mother had no desire to get well. Her doctor told me that, although permanently paralyzed, she was capable of walking again with a brace. But she rarely tried to stand up and never did her exercises. She was not interested in learning how to help herself. What she was interested in learning was how to use her sickness as a power over her husband and children. Finally, after years of rehearsals, she had been awarded the role she longed for: she was a Perfect Victim.

My father secretly assumed guilt for her illness. No one could deny that it was he who committed her to the psychiatric unit in the first place. He tried his best to rid himself of the guilt by passing it on to me. When guilt came his way, it was as if he held up a mirror and deflected it all my way.

I kept telling myself that my mother's illness wasn't my fault, but I didn't believe it. My mother didn't blame me. She didn't have to. All she had to do was to allow me to blame myself. I had been well-groomed for the role of Guilt-assumer. All my life I had collected guilt the way some children collect flowers or stamps. My parents helped me amass my collection by pointing out little delectables to me; like when my mother told me her doctor ordered her to drink a beer a day when she was pregnant with me because she was drastically underweight. She drank because of me, and I wasn't even born yet. The guilt my parents felt, for whatever reason, was too much for them, so they apprenticed me to the guilt trade. I served my masters well.

My mother used me as her personal maid, cook, companion, nurse, buddy, psychiatrist. I had to get her dressed and undressed, change her bedpan, make her phone calls, change the channel on the television, listen to her obsessive worrying about men and disease and money. I had to buy beer for her, so that she could get drunk and incoherent and weepy and fall out of her wheelchair. I would pick this limp dead-weight of a mother up off the floor and pour her into bed, while she slurred cliches about how she wanted the best for me and how she loved me more than life itself. Her room reeked of sweat and cheap perfume and bedpans and beer.

I would stumble dazed and numb into my bedroom, feeling like someone suffering from the aftereffects of having stuck a finger in a light socket. Then I would write a love letter to my girlfriend. The letterwriting was a daily ritual. It would always be a light, beautiful, loving letter, with tender and fragrant images of trust and devotion. But the real message was a desperate plea to love me and save me before my heart got so fed up with pumping bad blood to my insane brain that it simply stopped. This love was like antifreeze in my veins. These love letters to a girl I hardly knew were my daily reprieve from the numbness that would consume me each time I had to face my mother.

No one was there to tell me that this would not go on forever.

I managed to leave home. My father didn't like that. He came to my house that day, kidnapped me, took me back to my parents' house, beat me up, and cut all my hair off. I have been away from home ever since. That left no one home to take care of my mother except my father. No wonder he didn't want me to leave.

"You're killing your mother! You're breaking her heart!" he would say to me.

"Go ahead and leave, Dwight, I can make it. I'll survive somehow," my mother chimed in from her wheelchairthrone.

Physically I was gone from them. But emotionally I was still trapped in the house of horrors. The damage had been done, and it was extensive. I was nowhere near being able to fend off the blame. Standing up for myself had caused the cerebral hemorrhage in my mother. Being a bad son, I thought, had actually caused blood veins to pop in my mother's head. I felt evil and guilty and selfish. Just like my parents wanted me to feel.

I was free of their abuse and punishment, but the disease of blame claims revenge. I had to pay for the suffering and alcoholism I had caused them. So I began to punish myself. I punished myself with booze and pills and under-earning and shitfood and women destined to leave me. And I punished myself with solitary confinement in my own head. I felt like a leper with no colony. I felt like a single bean on a plate calling itself a meal. I began to kick my ass the way my ass had once been kicked by my father. I stole success from myself and amplified my failures. I denied myself a God. I denied myself a self.

And I denied myself a true love because I was afraid she would get sick on me and I would be trapped the way I once had been with my mother. I had managed to get away, but my father remained trapped in a sick relationship with my mother. He is her personal slave, catering to her every demand, unable to leave her alone for more than an hour at a time, giving her everything she needs except love. She knows he is trapped and she plays on his guilt for fear that he might become untrapped someday and abandon her. I see no love in his loyalty to her. Guilt and fear are his gods, and he follows their commandments. Both of them are stuck.

So I have this fear that a lover might get sick and I would become her eternal slave, tending to her needs and abandoning my own. And there is an equal fear that a lover might get well on me and I wouldn't know how to deal with her wellness because there has never been a well woman in my life. I feel stuck.

I want to get unstuck. I want to take a close look at the vast garden of sickness in my life, in order to discover what I can of the origins of the sickness. I want to see how these ancient feelings play themselves out in my life—to understand why when a lover gets a cold I feel like leaving town for a week, and why when someone gets sick I feel it's only to punish and manipulate me. I want to understand why when someone gets sick I want to punish that person. I want to understand why someone might not want to get well.

Rumor has it that there actually are people who get sick because they can't help it. And when they are sick they nurture themselves and allow themselves to be nurtured by loved ones. And they are grateful to the people who nurture them. And they in turn nurture their loved ones when it is their turn to get sick. And not all these people are carbon copies of my parents. And therefore they need not be treated as such. There is hope that I need not hide in my room when I get sick for fear that someone might see my weakness and vulnerability and abuse me. There is hope that these old patterns can be broken.

PARENTS

My mother was
 unable to give love
and my father was
 unwilling.
If they could've found
 a way to cash in
on emotional
 deprivation
they would have
 made a killing.

I WANNA GIRL JUST LIKE THE GIRL WHO MARRIED DEAR OLD DAD

I want a young girl
with light in her eyes,
a quick, two-pronged tongue
and believable lies.

a poet is an astronaut
taking pictures as the world
blows away...

ALONE

I am an astronaut
on a mission
outside the craft.
The rope
which connects me
to the craft
has been cut.
I spin off
into infinity.
I am alone in space.
This is no dream.
I am alone
floating
through space.

THE TRUTH FAIRY

One of my capped front teeth broke off. I was dental-flossing and it simply broke off and went flying across the room. My daughter was sitting in her bathtub when it happened. She thought it was a magic trick or something at first, until she saw the expression on my face and she said, "You look very upset, Daddy."

"I am upset," I told her. "My front tooth just broke off."

"Don't worry," she said reassuringly. "Just put it under your pillow."

I was quite a sight with the filed point of a tooth that the cap had once fit over staring back at me as I looked in the mirror. I took it quite well. I was grateful for that. I was also grateful that I had the six hundred dollars it cost for a new tooth. I was grateful that I had insurance to pay for half of that amount. I was grateful I had a dentist I could trust. I was grateful it didn't happen on a weekend and I was grateful I had an appointment the following morning. I was grateful there was no pain, even when I inhaled cool air or drank a cup of coffee. I was very grateful.

The following morning I was walking down the street on the way to the dentist and I was furious! I hated everyone and I didn't understand why. It was early in the morning and not much had happened. It was a pretty day. I had taken my tooth problem quite well. Then I began to realize maybe I had taken the problem a little too well. I looked for the source of the problem and became increasingly angry. Why? What was going on?

By the time I was seventeen years old I had seven caps and over twenty cavities filled. I spent a month in the dentist's chair. I did it because I was healthy enough to get the work done myself. One aspect of my parents' abuse was that they never took me to the dentist. They never taught me how to care for myself. A typical meal was frozen coffee cake for breakfast, canned spaghetti for dinner, and ice cream and candy in between. My teeth rotted out of my head.

Walking down that street, I felt that, after a lifetime of neglect and after over five years of recovery from my own alcoholism and drug addiction, I was still paying for their crimes of omission. I was glad that I could be grateful for this and grateful for that, but that was only part of the story. The other part of the story was that I had been extremely neglected by my parents and they had taught me how to neglect myself.

And now I am wondering when the price tag of this neglect will finally be cut from my sleeve. Just when I think I'm starting to do fine. Just when I think I have outdistanced my past, my teeth start falling out of my head. It reminds me of just how extensive the damage is. The wound is deep. Recovery is slow and difficult. Part of me is willing to accept that I might not ever fully recover from the devastation wrought by alcoholism upon my childhood.

But for today I do the best I can. I pick my tooth up off the floor and I walk to the dentist. I remember that gratitude is part of my salvation. And I search for the whole story. I look for the truth behind the tooth. I feel better now that I know why that tooth triggered such rage. And I wonder what would happen if I had put it under my pillow.

ALL POETS ARE QUEERS

Except for Robert Frost. He read at John Kennedy's inauguration. That is what my father told me. How doing a poetry reading at a political event can determine one's sexual preference is beyond me but I was young and desperate to believe that my father had at least a partial grip on truth.

I had a girlfriend and was very upset that I had to choose between her and poetry. If I wrote poetry would I become a homosexual? If I wrote poetry would I not have to shave for the rest of my life? Who wrote the famous odes to women?

And to think that up until that moment I had been writing poetry in the open and showing it to my teachers and girlfriends! Like a naked child without vanity I had been running around exposing what most people would keep secret. They all know about me! Why didn't anyone tell me?

I tried not to write but it was like never eating sugar. I kept having relapses, in private, of course. I would write poetry next to an open math book so people would think I was taking notes. I was a practitioner of clandestine poetry.

One day while rummaging through a closet I came across a cigar box. Without much thought I opened it, expecting to find partially used spools of thread or recipes never attempted. I found poems. One of them was about peeling off the skin of an orange only to find no meat inside and how that was like life. I closed the lid of the cigar box and slowly put it back exactly where I had found it, thinking all the while of a movie I had seen where a man was driving a truck full of nitroglycerine through snowy mountain passes.

"Oh! My God!" I said to myself, "My father must be a queer!"

DIGNITY

Treating people with dignity
doesn't come from without.
How can I treat someone with something
I don't know anything about?

To treat you with love
I must be loving of myself.
To treat you with kindness
I must be kind to myself.

I am the guardian of my spirit.
I am the keeper of a world within.
You are the destination of my love
but the world within is the origin.

I THINK MY FATHER WANTED ME DEAD

I think my father wanted me dead. I remember being told that the last thing they needed was a fourth child. But they quickly added that once they saw me they fell in love with me and changed their minds when they realized how wonderful I was. When they told this to me, I was a crippled child. I was crippled with a hip disease, and I walked on crutches for five years between the years of two and seven. If they didn't want a child in the first place, imagine how they felt about having a crippled one? I really didn't mind being crippled. I got a lot of candy handed to me by ladies in the grocery store. Being crippled also spared me from the beatings my mother and my siblings received. Even my father couldn't bring himself to beat a crippled five-year-old boy. At least not very often. But I evened the score for him. I felt so guilty that I had been spared, and I wanted so much to be a part of my brothers and sisters that, when I grew up and left my father and my crutches behind me, I began to beat myself with negativity and sensory deprivation and poor health and booze and drugs. Out of loyalty to my father, and empathy with my siblings, I picked up the whip and used it mercilessly on myself.

. . . . .

I once asked my father how I got my name. He said that when he heard I had been born he raced right over to the hospital. He was in the room visiting my mother, who had had a life-threatening, horrible labor—as she was prone to remind me over and over again. A nurse came in and asked them what my name was and my father chuckled nervously because he and my mother hadn't given it a thought. He looked down on the seat of a chair next to the bed and there was a *Life* magazine lying on it. On the cover was General Dwight David Eisenhower. My proud father looked up at the nurse with a patriotic gleam in his eye, and with the captain bars on his shoulders glistening in the fluorescent light, he said to her, "The name is Dwight."

I changed my name to Hannibal when I was fourteen years old. I lived under that name until I was thirty-four. It is still hard for me not to hate my name. But I have decided to live under the name I was given at birth. Because I didn't know that when I threw away my name, I threw away my identity with it. And I no longer will allow myself to be a co-conspirator in my father's assassination of my sense of self—and therefore of my right to live.

. . . . .

My father was drunk one night in the wee hours of the morning and he woke all his children and told us to get dressed because he was going to take us for a ride in the country. My mother saw a pistol stuffed down the back of his pants and she panicked. She gathered three of her four children and locked herself with them in the kitchen. All of the children were with her except me. I was left in the living room with my father who was pounding on the kitchen door and screaming threats at them. My father did not touch me. I am not even sure if he noticed me there. My mother eventually let my father in and I remember him beating my brother's head against the floor while holding him by the ears.

Why didn't my mother take me into the kitchen with her and the other children? Was it because I was offered to my father as a sacrifice? Did she offer up one child so that the lives of the others would be spared? Some animals do kill off their lame offspring so that those remaining have an easier time by not having to assist the gimpy one.

Why me? Why me, Mama?? Don't leave me out here! Let me into the kitchen, Mama! Let me into the world! Don't leave me alone out here with Satan! I'm only six and I want to be with you! Don't leave me.

. . . . .

My mother's first husband was killed in the war. She was left with her daughter and her boyfriend, who later became my father.

She married my father and he said to her one day, "Every time I look at your daughter I think of you having sex with your first husband. Get rid of her."

So she did. My mother sent her away to live with relatives. That child, my half-sister whom I never met, grew up and killed herself.

The threat of abandonment was very real for me. I knew about my half-sister at a very young age. I felt that my parents wanted me out of their lives and it was only a matter of time until I grew up and carried out the family tradition which dictated that we destroy ourselves.

· · • · ·

My father didn't have the courage to kill us, but he did manage to set us up to kill ourselves. And if we didn't die right away, then at least we were such abysmal failures that it was the next best thing. The important thing was that he looked good in comparison to us. But it is hard not to outshine a drunken loser. We had to keep our bellies real close to the ground and try real hard to fail, so that rare combination of bully and chickenshit, that handsome wife-beater, that uneducated genius in the art of perversion would feel like king-of-the-mountain when he was home. Any sign of our self-esteem was undermined. Any sense of humor was squashed. We were all given derogatory nicknames like Elf and Waldo. We were spiritually dismembered and scattered around the world. We were turned against each other so as to take the focus away from our parents. We still don't talk to each other. All ties were broken. Any semblance of trust between us was hacked to bits long ago. I don't even know what states my siblings live in or how old they are. My father didn't have the courage to kill us, so we were programmed to self-destruct.

· · • · ·

So here I sit in a London hotel. My face is handsome. My body is squeaky clean and I smell of sweet cologne. My clothes are fashionable (although they are mostly black and grey, the ACoA—Adult Children of Alcoholics—colors). I know how to make a living. I am a good parent. I am healthy. I am learning to love. And yet I feel that I am doing something wrong. I feel that by becoming healthy I am doing the opposite of what my parents wanted me to do—which was to die so that they could be self-pitying and grieve while being secretly relieved that they were free of the child they never wanted.

· · • · ·

I wanted more than anything for my parents to love me, and the message I got from them was they would love me most if I were dead. So I did the best I could, which was to roll over and play dead. But things are different now that I have taken over the job of parenting myself the way I was never parented. And I want very much for me to live. Even though I feel as if I am betraying my parents by doing so.

DEAR FATHER

It's such a shame.
I reach out to touch your heart
and my hand is engulfed in flame.

WHAT'S IN A NAME?

When I was fourteen I changed my name. No big deal. All the kids were doing it. There was Louis J. Lump, Snidely Bentwhistle, Gerhardt Bambi, and me, Hannibal Plath. We had fun with our new names and after about a week the other boys grew tired of the name game and dropped the pseudonym. Not me. I continued living under that name until I was thirty-three.

I knew the minute I pulled that name Hannibal out of a history book that it was more than a name. It was an identity. It was a way out of my alcoholic home. The person I was, Dwight Lee Wolter, was dying. He was evaporating like a drop of water in a hot skillet and he had to get out fast if he was going to make it. I had no hopes for Dwight's survival. He was getting clobbered in his home, didn't stand a chance.

But Hannibal was a conqueror. A survivor. He was immune. Immortal. Dwight could hide behind Hannibal and Hannibal would find a way out for them. And he did. But there was a price to pay. Dwight had to give his identity over to Hannibal and disappear.

It worked for a while. But Hannibal became as tyrannical as the parents Dwight was hiding from. And Hannibal turned out to be as frightened as Dwight was. To deal with the fear, Hannibal did exactly as Dwight's parents did. He chugged booze to flush down handfuls of pills. Years later Hannibal was lucky enough to become booze- and drug-free. But the wind had been taken out of his sails. He felt like the exposed Wizard of Oz.

One day Hannibal was writing a letter to a friend explaining how well his life was going since he quit drinking and drugging. He wrote "sincerely," at the bottom of the page and was about to sign it when he realized he didn't know what name to sign. He could feel his face go pale as he said to himself, "I'm writing a letter about how wonderful things are now. I'm four years without a drink. I'm living on Central Park West and have a family. But I don't know what my name is! I don't know how to sign my letter!"

I didn't have an identity. Dwight's parents killed Dwight. And booze killed Hannibal. There was no one left. I knew I had to go back to the beginning of my life and find the lost little boy who gave his identity over to Hannibal. That was the only place I knew to look in hopes of finding an authentic self.

I found the child alive but sick and lonely and hiding in a dark corner of my heart. I picked him up and cleaned him off and fed him. And I gave the child within me a name. I named him Dwight. And I am giving him all the love and respect he deserved but never got. Sometimes I miss Hannibal. He was an interesting fellow. But Dwight doesn't need him anymore. Sometimes I still think Dwight is too fragile to make it here in nasty ole Manhattan. But I'm giving Dwight all the hope and love I can muster. I'm giving him a chance. Dwight is back! Long live Dwight! I've got a name! I've got an identity! I've got a life!

NIGHT NIGHT, SLEEP TIGHT

I was almost asleep when I heard my bedroom door creak open and a sliver of light stretched across my face. I lay still and pretended I was not awake.

My father sneaked into my room. He knelt beside my bed. I felt him staring at me. I heard his heavy breathing. I smelled beer and brandy on his breath and in the pores of his skin. He gently ran his fingers through my hair and patted me on the head a few times. He leaned over the edge of the bed and kissed me once on the forehead. Then he did nothing. I could feel him staring at me again. He slowly stood up and sneaked back out of my room. I heard the door creak closed as the sliver of light retracted across my face.

My father was a mean and violent man. Yet when he slipped into my room to kiss me goodnight, an act he could never do when I was awake, I knew he loved me. This was the best he could do. I felt sorry for him. He was killing us slowly, but I felt sorry for him. I saw how pathetic he was. I knew he was killing us because he loved us. So unable was he to accept love, he had to kill all traces of love within himself.

I think my father felt sorry for me because I had to be his son. He knew I was a good boy. He knew I had done no wrong. He knew I was suffering at his hands. He knew he could not stop abusing me.

I think my father felt sorry for himself. He knew he and his son would never know each other, just the way he and his father never knew each other. The cycle of abuse and hatred was familiar to him, and he was powerless to stop it.

When my father left my room, I stared at the wall and tried to stuff my feelings deep within me, out of reach. He had showed love to me. But it was too late. I was only twelve years old, but it had already been years since I made a vow to myself that I would never show or feel love for him. I had killed my capacity to love before he could get to me, so that by the time he reached me I was already emotionally dead. I wondered if I was sad that my father was my enemy and could not be trusted. I wondered if he knew I was awake all along, and patting me on the head was just an elaborate trick designed to coax me out of myself so he could swat me like a fly as soon as my feelings landed on him. As numbness and sleep overcame me, I wondered if I would ever feel again.

HUNGER

I was lying in bed, reading. I was very hungry. I tried to ignore the feeling. Then pain of hunger and the noise of my stomach growling began to interfere with my concentration. I found myself reading the same paragraph over and over. I made myself lie there and keep reading. I battled giving in to the distraction of hunger. I knew the pain would soon subside.

I sat up. Where had I learned to do that? I realized that I had gone to bed hungry countless times as a child. Daddy was drunk. Mommy was getting drunk. Daddy was angry. Mommy was sad. I spent my childhood waiting to be fed. And rather than sitting alone at night in the blue light of television, eating cold potatoes and watching the news while my father was passed out and snoring on the couch in his boxer shorts—instead of that, I chose to go to bed hungry. I was hungry, but I had no appetite. It didn't seem so bad. I got used to it rather quickly.

I got out of bed and ate a banana. The pain went away. The growling went away. That was all it took. Amazing! My life had changed in an instant. I realized I didn't have to wait to be nurtured and cared for anymore. I could be the one to feed the hungry child within me. As a matter of fact I am the *only* one who can feed the hungry child within me. I'm not hungry anymore. I'm not waiting anymore.

I brushed my teeth, got back in bed, turned the light out and slept like a... like a... like a baby.

DANCING FOOL

For over five years I went to dances and was invariably asked by someone to dance, and I invariably told her the same thing, "I have never danced." The person would always say some variation of, "Well, why don't you make tonight the first time," and I would always say some variation of "no." What I would not say was that every time I went to a dance, I would hope that this would be the night I would try it. And every time I left the dance I would be depressed.

It wasn't that I didn't know how to dance. I dance all the time. At home. Alone. I'm a good dancer and I know it. But I also knew that the mere thought of dancing in public made me want to curl up in a corner. I don't know why. I made some intellectual stabs at the problem: extreme self-consciousness, fear of making a mistake, etc. And I also knew intellectually that my dancing is not that important to the other dancers. They are usually busy watching themselves and their partners or the band and are just not that interested in what I am doing. Despite my thoughts, the feelings persisted.

The other night I went to a dance, and a woman began to talk to me. I escorted her to the dance floor and danced one slow and one fast song with her. I felt like a little boy with a new bicycle. I excitedly told her that she was my first dance partner. I told several people about it, but of course no one quite knew the impact this breakthrough had upon me.

I danced with a couple of other women until the band announced the last dance, at which time about a hundred people placed their arms over the shoulders of the people on either side of them and in the form of one huge circle we danced the can-can. I was laughing and sweating and my heart was racing.

And in that moment I realized I felt a little guilty. I felt disloyal to my father, who never wanted any of his children to show any signs of excitement or light-heartedness or even any signs of life. I always wanted my father's love. I would do anything to "win" it, but I was sure that what he wanted me to do most was to be as miserable as he was. So I was depressed for him. And I acted like a tree for him. I had no fun for him. I impersonated his sickness until it became my own. I mimicked his negativity. I laughed at his racist, fascist jokes in hopes that my compliance would gain me admission into the private club of wackos who dwelled in his drunken head.

And then one night I found myself dancing him out of my life. I felt free. I felt dizzy. I felt defiant. I felt myself to be an equal member of the group. I was a link in a dance of life, doing the can-can for God as I whimsically told myself. And I felt wonderful. And I said a prayer of gratitude for my breakthrough.

The dance was supposedly over, but it certainly lived on in me as I rode my bicycle up Park Avenue at one in the morning singing and laughing along with my Higher Power and my sweet, sweet feelings—the sweet sensations of coming alive. Yeah, that's it, coming alive. Not reborn. For in many respects, I feel as if I have never lived. The sensation I feel is birth. I'm alive. I'm alive....

PART TWO

FRIENDS, LOVERS, AND OTHER STRANGERS

FRIENDS, LOVERS, AND OTHER STRANGERS

The way I was brought up by my parents provided me with no basis for successful intimate relationships with people. I accepted my parents' world view that this planet is a hostile place populated by people who can't be trusted.

I also learned not to trust myself. My sense of worth was constantly eroded by the steady application of the acids of their abuse. They blamed their children for their problems. And like loyal children, we accepted our parents' word as gospel. I believed that my very existence was enough to cause people to drink themselves to death. I have been unable to have a successful intimate relationship with myself because I hated myself for being the cause of so much pain in other people. My home also became a hostile planet, populated by a person who could not be trusted: me.

As an adult I chose to lavish my love on people who were incapable of loving in return. Using my lovers and bosses and friends as actors, I chose a cast of characters who would help me recreate my damaged relationship with my parents. It was a painful way to live, but at least it was familiar. I arrived at the first day of a relationship with suitcases packed with fear of intimacy, inability to say no, fear of the consequences of saying yes, fear of loss of self, fear of trust, fear of being used by yet another taker, and, yes, I even had fear of fear itself. I sought horrible people who frequented horrible places and with them I did horrible things which confirmed my horrible suspicions that life was horrible. No surprise to you, I would venture a guess, that my relationships were doomed before they began.

Here are some situations which illustrate my misguided attempts at connecting with other people—the desperate loneliness of a young man who wants to give and receive love but has absolutely no idea how. The realization of utter failure at having a meaningful relationship is indeed tragic. But I have come to believe that failure of my way of loving was a prerequisite to a change in the way I view the world, the way the world views me, and the way I view myself.

ODE TO MY BREAKFAST CEREAL

I have been fiercely loyal to my breakfast cereal for years now. Every morning I find myself pouring a bowl whether I want it or not. Sometimes I am bored eating it. Sometimes I resent eating it. But I eat it nonetheless. I have, I hope you understand, a tendency to latch onto things I like and stick to them, no matter what.

I am fiercely loyal to people as well. I find one person I like and I stick to her, no matter what. Every morning I find myself involved in that relationship whether I want to be or not. Sometimes I am bored with it. Sometimes I resent it. But I partake of the relationship nonetheless. It is as if the relationship is the only place where I can find nourishment. It is as if all my strength comes from this bowl full of love that comes from one box. There are so many varieties on the market shelves all priced similarly and in similar packages, yet I always walk straight to THE ONE as if no other choice existed. Some people believe that variety is the spice of life, but I remain unconvinced. I believe variety is the anxiety of life.

I am addicted to my breakfast cereal. I eat it. And eat it. And eat it some more. I cannot remember the last time I had fun eating breakfast. I eat only to survive. I try not to think about it. Sometimes I pretend I am really not eating at all. There is no longer a choice in the matter. The only alternative to you, my dear, is starvation.

PROGRAMMED
THAT WAY

When I walk out of my apartment
I always look to see
if I just missed a bus
before I look to see
if one is coming.
Why do I always
expect to see
something leaving me
and nothing on the way?

WHERE AND WHEN

Where do I end
and where do you begin?
Can I catch your attitude
like a cold?
Can this emotional virus
be isolated,
traced back to a germ
transmitted in the saliva
of an embrace?
When does your comfort
stop meaning more to me
than my own?
When do I stop trying
to fix you
when you're not broken?
When will I stop
reacting to you
and start responding to you?
When will I begin to trust you
and realize you are not
the women who came
before you?
When will I stop
missing you when I am alone
and wishing I was alone
when I am with you?
Where and when will be
the end
of my fear of tears?
When will I learn
to give and receive
compliments?
When will I stop
dragging yesterday into today
and pushing today into
tomorrow?
When will my expectations
be realistic?
When will I stop
responding to loneliness
by isolating myself
until the feeling fades into
numbness?
When will I stop
feeling I owe you my life
because you patted me
on the back
instead of thrusting a knife
into it?
When will I stop
responding with fear
to the offer of love?
When will I stop
accepting the unacceptable?

When will I stop
doing the same things
over and over again
and expecting different results?
When will I stop

the insanity of wanting insanity
back in my life?
When will I stop
seeking love from people incapable of loving?

When will I stop
the tragic misconception of
Dwight + woman = whole person
when the simple and elusive truth is
Dwight + God = whole person?
When will I stop
trying to get you to say I'm okay
so that I can then believe it?
When will I stop
offering love to people who
don't want it
so I can prove to myself that
the world is an unloving place?
When will I stop
turning to you for that which
I should turn to myself or to God?
When will I stop
thinking I'm dying of cancer
of the imagination?
When will I stop
thinking that if you don't love
me enough
then I have to try harder and harder
and that will make you love me?
When will I stop
feeling that if I make
my world real small
then I will be less
powerless over it?
When will I stop
mourning the loss of the childhood
I never had?
When will I stop...?
        When will I stop...?

When I'm good and ready,
that's when.

THRESHOLD OF PLEASURE

I was explaining to a friend how tough I am. Told him about the childhood I survived. Told him how when I was sick I would get up and walk to work when most people would call an ambulance to get them to the hospital. Told him how I get my teeth drilled without Novocain. Told him how I have survived two marriages. Told him how I laughed in the face of death. Told him how death laughed back. Told him about my incredible Threshold of Pain.

He said to me, "Now that I know about your Threshold of Pain, can you tell me a little about your Threshold of Pleasure?"

I tried to talk, but all I could muster was a small, gurgling noise. My friend noticed I was uncomfortable. He changed the subject and we never did finish the initial conversation.

The first time I tasted caviar, my immediate response was to spit it out. It was an intense, bizarre, and foreign experience. Often when I experience pleasure, my response is to spit it out. I have very little experience with pleasure, and it sometimes feels uncomfortable because it is unfamiliar. For someone who was raised by alcoholic parents, pleasure is an acquired taste.

Pleasure is scary stuff for me. Any intense sensation is scary, whether it is positive or negative. But in dealing with the negative, all I have to do is draw from my vast experience of failures, resentments, and broken dreams. I have always placed negativity in the same category as gravity. It grounds me. It keeps me from floating away. It is my anchor in a rudderless world.

I am afraid to feel pleasure because I cannot control it. As a kid I used to be afraid to laugh too hard because I thought, if I really got going, there was a possibility that I would not know how to stop. Last night at the circus with a friend I laughed so hard my face began to hurt. I had a hard time closing my mouth between laughs and my cheeks began to shake. My face felt like a mask with a smile stapled on it.

Pleasure takes some getting used to. Being raised in misery and neglect made me think that misery and neglect is what is expected of me. So I sometimes feel guilty when I am having a good time.

My parents' mood swings were so intense that episodes of pleasure were often followed by episodes of pain. It was as if pain was the price of pleasure. First you indulge in pleasure and then you owe the world some pain for it. So I was careful not to go too high up, so as to avoid the inevitable going too far down shortly after.

I take my pleasure in small doses now. I bite off small pieces and chew well. I allow myself to go off by myself after a pleasant experience and absorb the sensations. I whet my appetite for life and then I come back for more. I smile at the world and the world smiles back. There is no desperation or violence in my laughter. My Threshold of Pleasure is increasing as the quality of what I find pleasurable improves. I am beginning to enjoy life. And I feel life enjoys me. I am pleased with myself. What a change!

OPPOSITES ATTACK

My disease tells me that
that which imprisons me
will make me feel free.
It tells me that
that which will kill me
will make me feel like
I am really living.
The thought of
that which brings me down
makes me feel uplifted.
When I overeat I feel empty.
When I am hungry I feel full.
When I am in love I am
more conscious of being lonely.
When I am rich I hoard.
When I am poor I spend.
When I was drunk
I wanted to get sober
but couldn't.
When I am sober
I sometimes want to get drunk
but can't.

If opposites attract
you would think
I would like me
bcause I am myself
and I am my opposite.
The force that wanted me to die
was once stronger than the force
that wanted me to live.
The opposite is now true.
Neither opposite
has gone away.
They still stare each other down
across the long table of my spirit.
There is a force that
draws me to you
and a force that pushes me away.
Part of me moves toward you
as part of me moves away.
I am a juggler with life
in one hand
and death in the other
juggling so fast
they are a blur
traveling in a circle
around my head.

THE DIARY OF A YOUNG MAN WHO ONCE WAS ME

I am writing this book so that I can put together the puzzle pieces and try to figure out what the hell happened. One thing I thought that might be helpful was to go back to the love letters I wrote to my first girlfriend, which I have on file in my apartment. That I still have these letters on file after nineteen years of never having looked at them gives me some insight into the way I was.

I discovered a boy who was deeply in love with a girl he hardly knew. I was a good writer even then, and page after page testified to my true devotion to my first love.

One of the lines from a letter was, "If I buy the car that you want me to buy so that we can go out alone and not be dependent on a double date, then I won't have the money to buy all the clothes you want me to wear."

There was another letter in which I expressed gratitude for having a psychiatrist say I wouldn't be drafted for psychological reasons. I mentioned a dream I had in which "I was drafted and sent to Vietnam [it was 1967] and I got a 'Dear John' letter from you, so I stood up and let the enemy shoot me."

Another letter said, "In order to get along with me you will have to develop part of my philosophy of life, that being fatalism."

All of the love letters were riddled with negativity and severe depression and pain. There was a desperate need to be loved and I was willing to do and to be absolutely anything or anyone in order to 'win' my girlfriend's love. And 'win' is exactly what I had to do, because the girl was a promiscuous, beautiful, unavailable child of an alcoholic. In every letter I was trying to pry her out of the arms of another boy. I tried to force her to believe that everything was okay in our tragic relationship. The push me-pull you, come close-go away syndrome of the fear of intimacy already had a stranglehold on me at the age of sixteen. I seemed unable to be comfortable with the relationship unless I was trying to win her back or to keep her from going away. Everything was always my fault. My main problem was trying to figure out what I had to change about me so that she would love me.

I read the letters with compassion for the young man I once was. I thought, If that young man was my child I would put him on suicide alert. I would consider him to be very disturbed and rush him into treatment. I would do what I could to save his young life. But no one did that for me. Was everyone so caught up in their own troubles that they couldn't see me? Where were my teachers, my neighbors, my parents, my friends?

I realized that all the alarming traits I saw in that young man are still with me today. The neediness. The selling of my soul in exchange for a relationship. The fear of intimacy.

All these have been in me for the past nineteen years, since I wrote those letters. And if I weren't in recovery, I would be willing to bet that they would be in me for another nineteen years. Soul sickness remains as the body ages.

Now I have a chance to be free of the bondage of the past, or at least to recognize trouble before it plays itself out to such an alarming degree. I look forward to nineteen years of recovery. Writing this is part of how I hope to recover. I am not afraid to look back because I have so much to look forward to. I have respect for that young man and I have respect for me today.

MY RELATIONSHIPS

Come closer
come closer
come closer.

Not so close
not so close
not so close.

Where did you go
where did you go
where did you go?

Come back
come back
come back!

LOVE LOST

I was devastated
by the demise
of my marriage.
But it was not
because of love
lost
that I was
devastated.
It was because
of addiction
interrupted.

WHAT DOES WALT DISNEY HAVE TO DO WITH IT?

I hadn't seen her in fifteen years. Amazing how little she had changed. Different hair. A little more weight. Basically the same.

She recognized me too. I walked briskly toward her. Stopped in front of her. Took a deep breath with my mouth open like a swimmer about to go under and I said, "I'm sorry that I didn't announce your poetry reading."

"What?"

"I'm very sorry that I didn't announce your poetry reading!"

"I still don't understand what you're talking about," she said.

"Well, the last time I saw you I was giving a poetry reading and during the intermission you asked me to announce that you were giving a reading the following week. But I was so caught up in myself that I forgot to announce the reading and I'm very sorry!"

"That was fifteen years ago, Dwight!"

"And I've been sorry for fifteen years," I told her.

She laughed. I laughed. It would have been even funnier if it wasn't so true that I find it extremely difficult to forgive myself for even the slightest mistakes.

The last time I saw her was fifteen years ago and I was a twenty-one-year-old street poet with long, beautiful hair that looked like a lion's mane. I had a pocket full of pain that I carried around like a passport. I danced a slow dance with death to a sullen song which had no beginning and certainly no end. The melody just rolled over and over like a slinky down an endless flight of stairs. I courted numbness like an ultimate lover. But pain seeped in until I could no longer contain it. Like a single drop of turpentine trying to dilute a sea of paint, my numbness was ineffective against the pain. I screamed until I passed out. I woke up fifteen years later, brushed the dust off my vintage clothes, stumbled into the room, and saw her.

・ ・ ● ・ ・

That is why I remembered the conversation we were having fifteen years before. That is why I remembered the sentence we were on. It is as if nothing ever fades. Nothing goes away all by itself. Experiences left undigested just sit there in the stomach of my existence.

Like Walt Disney's body lying frozen at this moment in a vat waiting for a cure for death to be discovered, my unresolved feelings will wait forever for me to deal with them. They have the patience of frozen time.

・ ・ ● ・ ・

So I told her everything I just told you. She was just as accepting as you are right now. We see each other once in a while, and the past no longer interests us. It was a fun topic for about an hour. But the past is gone, resolved, digested. I hunger for a better meal. Here it is....

JUDGMENTS

I know I am judged by others
and my strongest resentment
is against people who judge me
on the basis of something
I secretly believe to be true.
But no one judges me
as harshly as I judge myself.
I live under the whip
of my own judgment.
I scrutinize the way in which
I drink a glass of water
(he gulped, he slurped,
a drop fell on his chin,
he didn't hold the glass
by the stem).
I judge the way I judge
(not witty enough,
I should have written
that one down).
All my judgments
stem from fear.
I use them to push
you away from me
and I use them to distance
me from myself.

It is at the point now
that when alone
I feel like I am with
a hostile stranger
who doesn't know
how to do anything right.
I'm tired of mimicking Daddy
and his vicious judgments
of me.
My judgments are like a thumb
clamped on the opening of a
balloon. If I let go
I fear the world will
spin off uncontrollably.

JUST JUMP!

A friend of mine went to a class where a group of parents were teaching their children how to swim. My friend commented on how a few of the fathers stood in the water while their children stood on the edge of the pool. The father would say something like, "Come on! Jump! Don't worry, just jump. Come on! Jump! What are you waiting for? Jump!"

When I was a kid, I would rather be shot in the head than to jump in the pool where my father was standing and waiting for me. There was one thing that was needed in order to jump and I certainly didn't have it and that was trust. Some madman standing in the water screaming at me was not what I needed to trust.

. . . . .

My parents built a house on an island. They did not teach me how to swim. Would you move to an island with children who didn't know how to swim? Why take a child who doesn't know how to swim and surround him with water unless you are willing to risk him drowning?

. . . . .

I finally learned how to swim by being thrown off a bridge by my best friend. I'm lucky I didn't drown and probably would have if the current hadn't pushed me toward shore. There was simply no one in my childhood I could trust.

. . . . .

I am an adult now and plenty of people have asked me to trust them and jump into their arms. I have not trusted a single one of them. Now I am lonely and unable to trust. I don't know how to keep my head above water in a relationship. I am afraid I will drown in your love.

VOWS

She married her father
I married my mother
then we proceeded to smother
the life out of each other.

STOOD UP

I was stood up by my date tonight. That hasn't happened to me since, well, last night. Two nights in a row by two different women. These women have never met each other. The only thing they have in common is me. I chose them both. I seem to have an abuse-seeking missile in my head that travels at the speed of light toward women who can't show up for me emotionally. It is not a conscious choice on my part to choose such women. There was no evidence, no indication that it would happen this way. But this disease, which manifests itself in dysfunctional relationships, is not a logical, rational disease. It seems that miles and miles beneath my conscious mind I still believe I need and deserve women who are totally unpredictable. I seem to need—not want, but need—women who are beautiful and concerned and confident and nurturing one moment and who, the next moment, apparently without provocation, turn into the emotional equivalent of drastically overcooked linguini. Where do I find these women? I am convinced that I have been trained by my ancestors for thousands of years for this role of human radar tracking down hostile humanoids. I am so sick of it! I am so hurt and tired. I don't want to fight. I don't want to get drunk. I don't want to read any more books on the subject. I just want to go to my dentist and have him shoot me up in the brain with Novocain.

And I also want to sit my Higher Power down on a chair across the table from me and ask him what the hell is going on. I'm not Jack the Ripper. All I wanted to do was go to a movie or a poetry reading, have a bite to eat and a nugget of small talk. I feel like the brunt of some cosmic, sick joke. Why me?

"Why not you?" I hear my stubborn Higher Power say to me in bass voice.

Okay, okay, what's the scoop, Doc? I need this lesson because of what? It's going to make me a better person and all that courageous bull? So God has a mission for me and I need to be strengthened, but why tonight? God rested on the seventh day and I haven't rested in seven years. Have you ever tried to go for a peaceful walk when with every step the pavement was pulled out from beneath you? My daughter says to me, "Daddy, when I call for you in the middle of the night you wake up so quickly it is like you were never sleeping!" I never sleep. I lie there and wait. I wait for marching orders from my Higher Power. And I feel like Job today. I felt like Job yesterday. But not the day before that.

I am still here. I am still a seeker. I still believe in the process. I still honor the will of God to the best of my ability. But I don't have to like it. I try not to need answers to the unknowable. I try to live on a steady diet of faith. But it is hard. I hurt. There is no one here to comfort me. Except God. And I am mad at him. I won't even capitalize the 'h' on him. I have no answer as to why I must go through this pain. There seems to be no resolution to this. There is no neat ribbon to tie up this bundle of nerves. I am tired of playing Aesop. My emotions are hanging upside down on a hook like a gutted calf in a butcher shop. And now I must shower and get on with my day. It is sunny out. I am taking my daughter to buy a Christmas tree.

CAFE ONE A.M.

drunk man eats pork
one hand on fork
other hand on hand

THE WET T-SHIRT

I clung to her
like a wet T-shirt
which soon grew
cold and clammy
she tried to
get me off her back
but I got stuck
up about her head
her arms pinned
next to her ears
she began to panic
the wet T-shirt
now tight against
her face like a
death mask
if you relax
I will slip
right off you
and you can
hang me up
to dry
and wear
someone different
for a change.

DO-IT-YOURSELF BIRTH

    I married my mother.
    I am growing up.
    I must seek food and air
       on my own now.
    She can no longer
       provide what I need.
    I am cutting
       my own
       umbilical cord.
    I feel the knife
       sawing back
       and forth
       across my life
       support system.
    I smell freedom.

RETURN TO THE WOMB

    going back
       going back
          going back
    desperately searching
    for what I lack
    missing some component part
    of my artificial heart
    running backwards toward the start
    is my way of crossing the finish line.

DWIGHT PLUS

The equation used to be
Dwight + Woman = Whole Person
but then the woman went away
and the equation changed to
Dwight + Zero = Zero.
It seemed that when the woman
went away and left me
I went away and left me.
I ran and found another woman
and the equation changed to
Dwight + Woman = Woman.
Things were getting worse!
Now even though I had a woman
it didn't mean I had a self.
So I went and found a God
and the equation changed to
Dwight + God = Whole Person.
And en route to finding God
I found a self so

Dwight + Dwight = Dwight

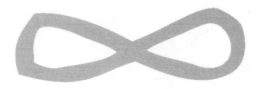

IT IS ONLY YOUR LIFE WE'RE TALKING ABOUT— WHY ARE YOU SO UPSET?

I went into my favorite bakery to buy a blueberry muffin. There was a huge tray full of them. They looked very similar, but I had my eye on the World's Most Perfect Muffin. The clerk asked me what I wanted and I said, "One blueberry muffin, please." Then I stood there, arms crossed in front of me, hoping that he would select the muffin I had my eye on. He didn't. There was nothing wrong with the muffin he selected, except that it wasn't the one I wanted. Therefore, everything was wrong with the muffin he selected. He placed the muffin in a white paper bag. I paid and thanked him. I walked out of the bakery and threw the muffin in the trash.

I was angry at myself because I hadn't asked for what I wanted. I was angry at myself because I was still hungry for a blueberry muffin. My guess is that the clerk would gladly have given me the muffin of my dreams had I only asked. *Only* asked, huh? I said to myself. That's like saying "only death." I felt incapable of asking for what I wanted. "So you're not perfect today," I said to myself in a schoolmarmish, pseudo-nurturing sort of way. "Besides, it's only a muffin." I did not feel soothed by this conversation I was having with myself. "But it is NOT *only* a muffin," the voice in my head continued. My whole life is like that muffin, and I am afraid to ask for it because I don't think I deserve the best.

Instead of asking for what I want, I hope people will be able to read my mind. I hope the clerk will say to himself, "This wonderful man doesn't seem very happy about his muffin today. I think I will ask him if the muffin I chose was the one he wanted." That isn't going to happen. I am disappointed to discover that here is yet another person who isn't a mind reader. So I throw him a few clues as to what I am feeling. I put on my depressed, pouty look. I tap my foot nervously when he reaches for the wrong muffin. I throw away my friendly facade and put on my threatening one so that he might become afraid to choose the wrong muffin. None of this works. This clerk is really an idiot if he can't decipher even my most obvious clues. I can't believe he is so callous. How can he treat me this way? No wonder I threw the muffin in the garbage.

Where did these feelings come from? I remember as a child asking for what I wanted but not getting it. Once in a while I would get something similar to what I wanted, but never exactly it. Eventually I gave up asking for what I wanted. I gave up asking for what I needed. My feelings and wishes were ignored by the people I loved. And if the people I love treat me with indifference when I ask for what I want, imagine what strangers will do.

When these feelings come up today I ask myself, "What would be the worst thing that could happen if I asked for what I wanted?" As a child the worst thing would have been to be beaten and abandoned. As an adult the worst thing would probably be that the person might say no. As a child, my belief that I had no right to anything except what was handed to me was so deep, I felt I would rather die than to ask for something. As an adult I can begin to see that I will not die if I stand up for myself. I might even be respected as a person who knows what he wants and is willing to go after it in an assertive and appropriate way.

I arrived at my job with blueberry muffins still spinning in my head. An employee showed up very late for work. I reprimanded him for being chronically late and let him know that the next time he did it he would be terminated. I noticed how much easier it is for me to *tell* someone to do something than it is for me to *ask* someone to do something. Telling someone they will be fired is quite easy. Asking someone for a muffin is not. Asking for something reminds me of my life as a passive, dependent child. I don't want to ask for anything, expecially help. I want to want nothing. I need to need nothing. But that is an impossible way to live. I want to trust that my needs will be met. I must learn that it is okay to want the best. I might not get it. But it is okay to want it. It is okay to ask for it.

Today I saw my world in a blueberry muffin. It used to be a lot easier to buy a muffin when it didn't represent some of my unhealthy attitudes. It is through microcosms of life that I see my recovery manifest itself. My behavior is beginning to change as I am willing to look at things differently. I am beginning to stand up for myself. I am beginning to avail myself of the goodness I deserve.

HOME

My phone won't work.
The doorbell is broken.
I waited three days
to call the repairman.

I am living
in a prison
of my own making.

Loneliness
is a person
who keeps me company.
I am very loyal
to this companion.

Once in a while
I rattle the bars,
not to loosen them,
but to make sure
they are firmly
in place.

I WENT AND BOUGHT A BOTTLE

I went and bought a bottle
of your favorite perfume.
I put some on my pillow
and I sprayed it around the room.

I went to our favorite restaurant
and I asked for another chair.
I poured a drink into two glasses
and pretended you were there.

I went and got a girlfriend
who reminded me of you.
That's the only kind of woman
that I am attracted to.

I know it isn't fair to her
and it isn't fair to me,
but no matter into whose eyes I look
yours are the eyes I see.

It seems no matter where I go,
no matter what I do,
nothing can free me from the wish
of being back with you.

IN LOVE WITH LOVE

I'm in love with love. I enjoy walking around like Hamlet: melancholic, slightly frustrated, longing for my true one. I stroll the beach at sunset, gazing to the sea, wishing there was someone there with me. But if that person were to arrive, I would get defensive and withdrawn. It is the illusion that attracts me, not the reality. I want what I can't have. The rabbit, the carrot, and the stick. The fox and the grapes.

LULLABY

Here is what you do. Take three popsicle sticks and bind them together with tape. Then wrap a large amount of gauze around and around the top half of the stick and tape it securely to the other half of the stick so the gauze won't fall off. Now take the whole thing and tape it to the wall just above my side of the bed. If I have a convulsion put that thing in my mouth. Not too far into my mouth. I don't want to choke on it. Put it just far enough in to keep me from swallowing my tongue. Don't be afraid. It's not that big a deal. And whatever you do, don't give me a drink. Goodnight, sweetie.

HUMPTY DUMPTY

My girlfriend said that since we broke up there has not been any alcoholism in her life. My belief is that the disease in her began long before she met me and it will continue long after I'm gone. I was a set-up for playing a part in her life—a part determined by her father's alcoholism, as she began to recreate the family drama in which she felt so much at home. And the next relationship she has with a man, even if he is not an alcoholic, will be an alcoholic relationship, because she is an untreated adult child of alcoholics.

Saying and feeling this absolves me of a lot of guilt and responsibility I feel for inflicting alcoholism on her, when, in fact, she was desperate for it. She followed me across the country in search of it. And my becoming the object of her obsession with her father damaged me greatly. It kept me from recovery as long as I was playing my role in her unresolved childhood-revisited family drama.

Like Judy Garland, who grew up and could no longer play the part of Dorothy, I grew up in recovery and could no longer play the part of her father. So all of a sudden our relationship had a great fall. And all the enabling horses and all the enabling men couldn't put it back together again.

HER

If I love you
and you don't love me,
that makes me
want to love you more.

If I only would love you
more and harder and longer,
then maybe I could
make you love me.

I love all the mommys
dressed up like girlfriends
and wives.
I see their hatelove coming
before they open the door
or their mouths
or their legs.

Problem is,
I judge them guilty
of a crime about to be committed
or a crime committed years ago
before I met them.
Never looking at the woman,
I look at her ancestors, her
bloodline, study her family tree
for inherent ability to abuse me.

A dark mysterious lanky
poor beautiful trapped
talented stoic isolated
musty painter, Soho-type,
who lives with no friends or pets,
is best for me.
This rare breed of woman
really knows how to
not love me back.

HERE'S LOOKING AT YOU, KID

I look at me by looking at you.
I see in you what I see in me and can't accept.
I hate your arrogance and pride because
I hate my arrogance and pride.
I accuse you of my shortcomings.
I condemn in you my guilt.
I punish you for my sins.
I don't respect my friends because
if they like me they suffer from poor taste.

I miss you because you are so cold
and it reminds me of the coldness in myself.
Your inability to love me
reminds me of my inability to love myself.
If it hurts this much it must be love.
Please don't take my pain from me.
It's the only thing I know.

I could never get close to you.
I mean I could never get close to me.
I mean you never loved me.
I mean I never loved me.
You have been disloyal and unfaithful to me.
I mean I have been disloyal and unfaithful to myself.
Who are you, anyway?
Who am I, anyway?
Is there an echo in here?

VALENTINE'S DAY

Tonight it is Valentine's Day.
There is a light snow falling
which turns to water
upon impact with the pavement.
I want to rent a car
and drive around New York
splashing all the couples.

HOTEL

Everyone at the hotel knows Bert Wilson. He has lived silently alone in the same buck-a-day room for twenty years. Every day you can find him sittin' at the end of the bar near the men's room. He's the one who makes a clinkin' noise every time he talks which ain't too often. The bartender says it's his upper false teeth clinkin' against his lowers that make all the noise.

Anyway, one night I was helpin' old Bert up the stairs like I do every night and he said he wanted to take a shower and I wasn't about to complain 'cause I know for sure he ain't had one for at least two months so I got him a towel and soap and went back downstairs to my beer before anyone else drank it. About 1 A.M. I went upstairs to go to sleep (I was yawnin' like crazy) and I heard the shower still runnin' but that wasn't nothin' special 'cause Bert always leaves it on and I always end up turnin' it off for him. When I got to the door I found out it was locked and I got kinda worried. Bert was in there for three hours. I started bangin' against the door like crazy. I mean like I didn't even know I still had that much strength left in me and my shoulder started hurtin' like crazy but I kept on bangin' and yellin' his name.

Finally the bartender heard all the commotion and got scared and came runnin' upstairs with this old gun he keeps behind the bar just in case if you know what I mean and when he saw what I was tryin' to do he told me to stand back and he shot the handle off the door. When we got inside we saw Bert lyin' on the floor and I knew I mean I just knew he was dead and I took his head in my lap and started prayin' cause I didn't know what else to do and I figured if God was anywhere I hoped he was there with me then. I slapped Bert's face a few times and I saw him move and I started sayin' real loud, "Thank God...thank God."

Bert opened his eyes and looked around like he was tryin' to remember where he was and he finally said, "I was dreamin' (click) that I was lyin' in a big meadow of flowers and weeds and grass and bugs and (click) dirt and this rain was fallin' on my head and it felt like little fingers (click) runnin' all over my body." I stared at him and I didn't know what to say until my mouth dropped open and all I could muster was, "You damn fool, you wasn't in no meadow you was dead drunk lyin' on the bathroom floor and you caused us a whole lot of worry" and all he said was, "Oh yeah, well next time (click) I'll drink a little harder."

HYDE PARK

They really do come for Hyde Park Corner Sunday speeches and some bring their own boxes to stand on (those who can still stand on boxes, that is) and some wear ties and some don't wear shirts and some whistle S's through their rotten teeth and some don't have any teeth at all. Some have disciples easily won with a drink and some hate Americans and some are Americans and some are soldier musicians without all their fingers. Some can't remember who they are and some can't forget and some simply don't care. All are poets running out of time. Some are second-generation bums whose bubbles burst and dropped them hard on Hyde Park Corner on this Sunday afternoon, where they spend themselves grubbing attention from tourists who don't want to be touched—only amused—by little puppet people with charming English accents.

I'M BACK

I am back in New York.
I wash the soil of London
off my hands and say good-bye
as it gently swirls
down the drain.
I smell the English rain
in my bag of dirty laundry.
It is dinner time in London.
All my friends are eating
without me.
I want to go back.

TIME TO CHANGE

If we both look at our watches
and we show different times
I will set my watch to yours.
I could have a Seiko.
You could have a Bulova
that has been dropped
in the toilet three times.
I will set my watch to yours.
If we both look at our hearts
and we show different feelings
I will set my feelings to yours.
Your feelings could have been
amputated from the neck down.
Your heart could have been
dropped in the toilet three times
but I will set my feelings to yours.
Such is my need to believe in you.
Such is the extent to which
I fail to believe in me.

THE SEIKO SYNDROME

You wear a Seiko?
I wear a Seiko too!
You have an "O" in your last name?
I have an "O" in my last name too!
You live on the ninth floor?
I live on the ninth floor too!
You're an orphan?
I'm an orphan too!
This relationship was clearly
meant to be.
Won't you come and live with me?

LOVE !!!

Quaaludes were my drug of choice
and I took them.
I was her drug of choice
and she took me.
I took them
and she took me.
It was a marriage
made in a laboratory.

SHARING

Obsession,
like mold,
grows in the shade.
Exposed to light,
it withers.
Talk about it.

LOSE / LOSE

Because you don't get
exactly what you asked for
then anything else I do
is not enough.
I will be judged
by how far I fall short
of the goal you set for me.
Whatever I have done
does not count.
It is what I did not do
that really matters.
I'm damned if I do
and damned if I don't.

        I deserve better treatment than this.
        I may not get it from you
        but I might get it
        from myself.
        Anything worth doing
        is worth doing
        badly.

Who are you to
set my standards for me?
I do my best
and if that isn't good enough
for me
then I lower
my expectations.
That way I win
if I'm perfect
and I win
if I'm not.

DREAM NO. 93

I couldn't find my socks. I knew Jane knew where they were. I found Jane in the back seat of a car with a musician with whom she had an affair when I was out of town. There were a bunch of other people in the car and they were about to pull away from the party.

I ran to the car and put my head in the window and moved my mouth close to Jane's ear and said loud enough for everyone to hear, "When we made love a little while ago I lost my socks. Can you tell me where they are?" She said, "No."

My intention was to let the musician know that Jane was mine and he should, therefore, not touch her. He was unaffected. Jane was unaffected.

As the car pulled away I told myself that the humiliation had been all worthwhile because I had been able to press my lips next to Jane's ear once again and I had been able to feel my face in her nest of hair. I settled for so little.

I watched them cuddling and laughing as the car pulled away. I turned to go back to the party and saw the lawn and the house were empty. The windows were all broken out. The pool was dry and the bottom was cracked. Weeds were waist high and ivy had grown halfway up the walls.

I turned back toward the car and it was gone. I stood in the middle of an empty field without even a breeze to keep me company.

MY FAVORITE THINGS

The smell of newspapers,
pencils and tweed.
The taste of suspicion,
sex and greed.
These are a few
of my favorite things.

The glare of cold, wet marble
in a young woman's eyes.
The allure of fear, lies,
regret and alibis.
These are a few
of my favorite things.

The agony of victory
and the thrill of defeat.
Feeling abandoned
the day after we meet.
These are a few
of my favorite things.

Is the stuff of yesterday
all that tomorrow brings?
I've had enough
of my favorite things.

YOU

I am a poet
made out of paper.
You are a paperweight
that keeps me from
blowing away.

KEEPING IT GREEN

If my world got any smaller
it would become invisible
it would be as small as
an ice cube
melting
in a glass of gin
the ice cube
I used to talk to
the one that talked back
in constantly fading
whispers
both of us
getting smaller
by the minute
telling each other how
big we would be
if we could just
get out of this
damn glass.

THE 'F' WORD

It's taboo,
strictly
sinful.
Only weaklings
indulge in it.
It's messy and
unmanageable,
primitive and
indiscriminate.
It can ruin your
reputation.
Don't let your
parents find out
you're having
FUN.

THIS WORLD AIN'T BIG ENOUGH FOR THE TWO OF US

There is not enough love
in this world
to meet my needs.
Not even heaven above
holds enough love
to suit my greed.
I have a thirst
no drink can quench,
a hunger no food can kill,
an itch no hand can scratch.
Like the black hole,
free-floating through the
universe,
I consume everything
in my path,
including light,
and writing this
makes me hungry.

TO LENNY BRUCE

as you lay dying
a chain of images
waiting for the
mortician
your mind sliding down
America's banister
I think of actors
fighting for your memory
on Broadway
actors
who wouldn't return
your phone calls
as you lay dying
I think of newsmen
idle hands in the pockets of Time
viewing your death
as Moment in History
when you lay
smiling face
bareass
on the bathroom floor.

FAT FRED

Fat Fred never cared. He ate too much and talked too much and played a lot of chess. He drank a lot too. One balmy Sunday night I was walking down the street when I saw Fred lying in the gutter. I tried to help him stand, but forklifting three hundred pounds of unwilling matter is not easy. I finally gave up, put a dime in the parking space he was occupying and walked on.

THE GLASS BOX

The bathroom of her very small apartment is directly across from the front door. In order to let me and my bicycle out, she had to stand in the bathroom, holding the door open by the handle, waiting for me to pass. On the way out, once the front wheel had cleared the threshold, I looked back. I was in the light of the passageway. She was in the darkness of the bathroom. I saw her white moon of a face pressing out of the darkness. She was only two feet away. Two feet away. Yet she seemed as distant to me as...yes...as the moon.

Her face was bright, with hazy borders. She was so deep within herself, it was as if there was some spiritual vacuum in her head that was sucking the tears back into her eyes. I hate to say it, but her face was like a death mask. It reminded me of a famous photograph of the Shroud of Turin.

She was looking at me across centuries of remoteness. Her dry lips were vast fields of forgotten wheat. Her hair hung like vines in a forest never visited. She was like the black hole in the universe that eats light. She was beyond the reach of even sadness, wrapped in layer after layer of night.

I had come to find her. I peered and searched. I sat still and waited. I spoke. I was silent. I listened for a flapping of wings. I listened for the sound of water splashing. I listened for her breathing.

I found no one. Was I looking for unicorns again? I don't think so. I was looking for a last chance. I was looking for a single note in a world full of song. I would have settled for a sigh in a world full of sorrow.

I found a glass box with potential locked inside. I walked around it and around it. There was no key, and no door if I had found a key. A glass box full of potential where most people carry a heart. It was glowing and warm. But that didn't help much.

A glass box. A white moon of a face. I went home.

BIRTHDAY

And so it is my birthday and so I'm alone
and I haven't a candle and I haven't a home.
I haven't a lover and I haven't a wife.
I haven't a party, but I have a life.
Yes, I have a life.

After a lifetime of settling for less,
I have become my own best friend.
I am the friend I have been waiting for.
I do not have to wait for the arrival
of cards that have never been mailed.
I mail myself a card. I show up for me.
I am on my side. There is no need to
run and hide from the memories of no one
being home, no one calling on the phone.

I want to be loved today. But there is no
one here to love me. So I will love myself.
All I have to do is figure out how.

I went to a bakery, the nicest in town.
I bought myself a birthday cake.
I came home and put a candle in it.
Lit it. Turned the lights out.
And I sang Happy Birthday to myself.
I sang soft and slow. I made a wish.
I blew the candle out. I felt foolish.
I am glad I did it. I hope I never
have to do it again. But I am glad
I did it.

PART THREE

TO PARENT

TO PARENT

How can I be a successful parent when I was never successfully parented? The beginning of the solution was to learn to parent myself. That was no easy task It is like saying the beginning of successful brain surgery is to perform brain surgery on yourself. When all you have known is abuse, it is a long and difficult process to learn to love and respect and nurture yourself. But I am doing it.

The self-love I am learning is moving out into the lives of other people, like waves emanating from the point where a pebble is dropped into a calm lake. Self-love begets love of others.

My five-year-old daughter is very different from the way her father was as a child. She is warm and outgoing, calm, willing to take risks, secure in the knowledge that she will not be punished for mistakes. She knows she has rights. She is proud of her work. She feels like an important person whose contributions are appreciated.

My daughter is the hope of her ancestors. It is too early to tell, but she appears to represent a break in the long arm of alcoholism and madness that has reached with its snarly fingers into the souls of our family for hundreds of years. I am not trying to live my youth through my daughter. My youth is gone. It never happened. It is unfortunate that the dysfunctions of my family deprived me of my childhood. But I am grateful that I was not so damaged as a child that I am unable to become a good parent. My parents must have done some things right. And I must be doing some things right. The goodness of the father is visited upon the son. My daughter is doing very well. I feel like I am learning to love through her. Hers is a pure and unconditional love. She has a basic belief in the fundamental goodness of people. She is not naive. She knows that evil and danger exist, but that is not the focal point of her universe. She is not fixated on the negative the way her father was. The moment my daughter was born and she opened her eyes I was the first person she saw. The first words I said to her were, "You are a child of God and you have been placed in my care. You do not belong to me and never shall. Welcome to your life. I am here to love you forever."

Living up to my commitment to my daughter has led me to a new and better way of loving other people. I am still a flawed human being. And the fear in me is great. But love is lessening the fear of living. I am watching a child grow and prosper in a difficult world. I gain strength and faith through a five-year-old girl. Through her I am learning that childhood is painful no matter who your parents are. Being part of her life is helping me become reconciled to my past and get on with the rest of my life.

BIRTHPOEM

Sleep is what I thought
the night was up to.
We lay routinely in bed
as the full moon turned
the tidal waves within
your mother's belly.

Get up. Trace the source of the
discomfort. Chart the times at which
the waves lap at your mother's shore.

Zoe reclines on the red sofa which looks
as if it's been waiting for this occasion.
She listens to Celeste Sophia
tapping at the threshold.

I put on my favorite robe,
weave new caning into the
dining room chairs, glue a
coat hook onto the bathroom door,
making room for one more coat,
doing all the things I meant to
have done by now for your arrival,
as if your little heart cared
about robes and chairs and caning.

Your mother erupting now
rumbling with rumors
of long awaited arrival.
The moon massaging
her globe of a belly.

Where are the promised waters?
Who decided they would flow
at this hour of deepest night
when the best of poems are born?

Contraction begins.
Take a deep, cleansing breath.
Blow the pain away.
In the room where your mother
labors, I open Venetian slats.
Moonlight streaks make stripes
across your bellyhome.
I slip slivers of shaved ice in Zoe's
parched mouth, arid from birthchants,
stroke her face with a cool cloth,
fan her with my breath,
getting closer and closer to her until
we breathe together, contract together,
sigh and relax together.
My flesh vibrates.
My ears hum.
The sound of blood pulsing
through my veins is deafening.

We're in transition,
shaped by birth rites of initiation
into different people.

We are your parents now.

So this is what it is like
to live and sponsor new life,
which will live and sponsor new life.
It seems so simple now.
I was learning from you,
my celestial one,
our celestial wonder,
before you were even born.

THERE IS

There is peace in this room.
There is peace in me.
There is peace in eternity.
There is eternity in me.

NOTES TAKEN DURING CELESTE'S FIRST YEAR

Before the first poet
wrote the first poem
the poet's mother
gave birth to the poet
who gave birth to the poem.

I look over my shoulder
and there is a likeness
of myself
watching
me write this.

That likeness has a name
and the name is Celeste
and she is the best
girl on Central Park West.

I sit at the typer
wringing my mind dry
yearning for the Muse.
Celeste reaches up
to the keyboard
and joyously bangs
on the keys.
I think she is trying
to tell me
that this process
is less mysterious
than I suppose.

She has so many things to say
yet not one thing is a word.
She speaks in a language
only angels can understand.

Her mind is constantly roving
as she studies the bizarre
function of a toothbrush
and savors the delicate taste
of an aged shoestring.
She moves through life
kissing light sockets
and speaking politely
to refrigerators.

It is the eve of Celeste's
first birthday.
I think of her lying
in her crib
huge by the standards
of one year ago.
I think of the marvelous
things she has done.
When she was one day old
she doubled her age
in just twenty-four hours.
And one year from tomorrow
she will have doubled her age again.

One day I cradled her
as if she were so fragile
she would break
if I breathed on her.
She was too weak
to lift her head from the pillow.
It seems to me now
like it was the next morning
I walked into her room
and saw her standing in her

schoolbus yellow crib
wearing red bib overalls
rattling the rails.
I take things like standing
and lifting up my head
for granted. It took
Celeste to teach me gratitude
for so many simple things.
I am growing into my gratitude
as she is growing into those
red bib overalls.
It seems like
everything in our lives
is beginning to fit.

For the past year, Celeste,
I have wanted to ask you
many questions. But
I have learned to accept
your silent answers.

Will you try to remember
and tell me at some later date
if I still want to know
what you dreamed of
when you were three days old?
Did your feet seem miles away?

It has been quite a year, my dear,
full of learning and changing.
Sometimes it seemed too fast,
yet everything happened
when it was supposed to.

You walk now.
You're learning to talk
now, learning to push out on
the wall of your world now.

I have the honor of being your
father. I want to thank you
for this opportunity to become
something greater than myself.
I feel connected to life again.

Walk on my little celestial wonder,
walk on. The journey is not easy but
I promise you it is worth it.

I have given what I have to offer.
I will share with you what I can.
The rest is up to you and your God.
The world is in your tiny hands.

WE ARE TWO, SO WHAT DO I DO?

Since I am the child of alcoholics
and since I am the youngest in my family
and since I was an alcoholic and drug addict
in adolescence and early adulthood
and since I have no wife to turn to for help
I find I must act as if I know
what the hell I am doing
in the raising of my daughter.

I am convinced it takes three to make a family
and we are two so what do I do?
I can tell she is doing well
but sometimes I feel it is just luck.

There is no precedence for recovery
in my family.
If we were talking about sickness
I would have all the answers.

I guess I will ask for help
although it goes against every cell in my body
because it breaks the code of silence
that if broken is punishable by abandonment
but what the hell I was already abandoned years ago
by parents who say they raised me
but the truth was I grew rather
like a dandelion at the edge of the road
and I was abandoned most recently by a woman
I chose specifically because she didn't know
how to love and I didn't love her either
but boy was the scenario familiar.

But we must be doing something right
because my daughter appears to be a break in the
chain of alcoholism that has been wrapped around
my family for zillions of years.

What I am finding so difficult to say
is that I need help raising my daughter
and I am scared I will mess her up
although every indication is that
I am doing a great job.
But I am scared and I need help.

SICK KID

I should be home, drunk, beating my kid. At least that is what the statistics say. Abused children of alcoholics grow up to be abusive alcoholic parents.

Instead, today I stayed home from work to nurture my sick daughter. I gave her medicine, cold baths, a ripe plum when she was feeling better. I read her books, talked to her, was there for her when she fell asleep and when she woke up.

She had feverdreams of blankets racing through the room. I turned on the fan and she hallucinated about it spraying bugs all over her. She screamed and tried frantically to brush them off. So I turned the fan off and fanned her instead with a book of rhymes.

She said she thought she was going to die. I promised her she wasn't and she said, "How do you know? What if God says 'Celeste, I want you dead'?" I talked to her about life and death, gradually changing the subject to playgrounds and stuffed animals, as her tired, milky eyes watched my lips form words she didn't understand.

I sat with her, running my fingers through her hair, watching her until her eyes closed and her breathing slowed and she fell into a comfortable, although feverish sleep.

A memory of my own childhood cut through the gauze-wrapped years until it landed like a piece of contaminated food in the pit of my stomach. I remembered being a child, about my daughter's age, in a hospital in Japan, under observation for a mysterious leg disease. My parents checked me in. It was early afternoon. They left, saying they would return that night.

The sun set. I sat up in bed, looking through the window slats out onto a parking lot, watching for my parents' car, and sobbing. A kind nurse went off duty, and a cranky one came on. She reprimanded me for my sobbing many times. A few hours later she came in, snapped the window slats closed, and turned off the lights.

"Stop sobbing! Act your age! Your parents aren't coming, and even if they did, they wouldn't be allowed in. It's nine o'clock. Visiting hours are over. So stop crying and go to sleep!"

She left the room. I slid down in bed. I stuck a corner of the pillow into my mouth. It tasted like bleach and illness. It muffled the sounds as I cried myself to sleep.

I didn't walk for the next five years.

The memory and the feelings left me like fumes being sucked out of a restaurant kitchen. I looked down at my sleeping, sick child.

I am learning to love. I don't know where it is coming from. I was raised by troubled parents. I am the youngest child and a single, male parent with no previous experience with children. I have no spouse to turn to for help or advice. All my love relationships have been seriously flawed.

And yet, somehow, despite what I have been through, I am learning to love. I love and nurture my daughter the way I was never loved and nurtured. I can't imagine anyone doing a better job. I am fantastic. I am an excellent father.

I am grateful. I am changing from the cold, hard, emotionally closed man I once was. I want to remember I said this. I am coming alive.

FEELING STUCK

It is not easy being stuck indoors all day with a sick five-year-old. I should know. Not only am I a parent to one. But I've been stuck with a sick five-year-old in my head for the last thirty-one years.

HOUSEKEEPING AS A SINGLE MALE PARENT

When the dust balls
that blow across
the kitchen floor
grow too large
I pick them up
eventually.

PARENTING MYSELF AND MY DAUGHTER

How can I be a decent single parent?

That was the question which confronted me when I staggered out of an unsuccessful marriage and found myself with joint custody of a two-year-old girl. I had been raised by parents who were not good for their children in many ways, not the least of which was their inability to be emotionally supportive of us. I was also the youngest child in my family and I had no experience with children. Presently, there was no wife, mother, or girlfriend to turn to for help and advice. My task was to, somehow, learn to love and nurture my daughter the way I was never loved and nurtured. I was brought up believing that the nurturing of a child was a woman's job. Now I had to assume both roles, that of being the nurturer (Mommy) and the discipliner (Daddy). I had to be the breadwinner at home as well as the grocery-buyer for the school fair. I sometimes had to give up my chair at management meetings in order to take a chair in the pediatrician's waiting room. I knew I had to become a Daddymommy without virtue of knowing what a good Daddy or a good Mommy is. There had been an absence of role models in my life to guide me. I was not encouraged by statistics that say that poorly parented children grow up to be lousy parents.

I don't want to blame my parents for my problems. I am an adult and I want to take responsibility for my life. I don't want to get stuck in blame and anger. But part of accepting responsibility for myself is to determine who is accountable for what. All my life I had successfully avoided blaming my parents for anything because I simply couldn't handle looking at what had happened to me as a child. I certainly didn't pin all my problems on my parents. But I eventually took a searching and fearless look at where some of my behavior and character defects originated. I had to be willing to look at the things my parents had done right as well as the things they had done wrong, so as to get a balanced perspective of what went into the making of the person I am today. I tried to pin the tail on the donkey and say: this is what happened. This is what it felt like. This is how the way I was raised still plays itself out in my life today.

I discovered that a lot of my character defects are a result of the way I was parented. Holding my parents accountable allows me to see how a problem might have originated with them, but now it is I who perpetuates the problem by not taking responsibility for changing it.

A huge obstacle to holding my parents accountable for their parenting is my denial; I deny how difficult my childhood was. My most frequently used tool of denial is letting my parents off the hook. I let them off the hook even if it means I have to put myself on the hook in order to do it. I put myself on the hook by blaming myself the same way they always blamed me. I let them off the hook by finding some fault in myself that caused them to behave the way they did. I would tell myself, for example, that if only I had been a better son then they would have been better parents. As an adult I put myself on the hook by telling myself that I am merely an ungrateful blame-seeker, who won't let go of the past and continues to needle the two people who loved him the most. Closer to the truth is that I have a desperate need to believe that those two people were better parents than they were. I don't want to face the fact that they were not there for me emotionally. I don't want to admit that my parents often acted in disregard of my well-being. I don't want to admit it because it hurts too much. I was treated with little respect by parents who had little respect for themselves. They had low self-esteem and they taught low self-esteem to their children. They couldn't love because they had never been loved. They simply didn't know how to do it.

And, lo and behold, I found myself in the same situation with my daughter as my parents found themselves in with me. I had to act as if I knew what the hell I was doing in raising my daughter. I joined an organization of single parents and began to ask for help. I joined another organization which deals with the problems of adults who were raised in dysfunctional homes. There I learned that the feelings of pain, loss, perpetual disappointment, and fear of intimacy do not simply go away. They had remained lodged in me like a fishbone caught in my throat. I had to allow myself to feel those painful feelings which I had tried so hard to avoid all my adult life. I had to learn to talk about them with understanding people.

I learned that becoming a better parent would begin by parenting myself in the way that I was never parented. I had to acknowledge the existence of the child within me, the little boy inside the man, and I had to give that child all the love and respect he deserved but never got. The beginning of being good to my daughter was also the beginning of being good to myself. It is no small job.

Living up to my commitment to my daughter has led me to a new and better way of loving other people and myself. My dual role of Daddymommy has allowed me to embrace the feminine as well as the masculine sides of myself. Consequently, I feel I am a more whole person than I was in my marriage. Then I leaned on a woman to provide the caring for our child, which I felt incapable of simply because I am a man. I am a single, male parent, yet I have achieved a marriage of love and logic, of empathy and discipline. I lift weights at my health club and then go shopping for my daughter's panties and stockings. I supervise a staff of fifty men during the day, and cook meals and bathe my daughter at night. I have discovered that I am more flexible than I ever suspected. And more loving.

I can see now that because of my painful past, I have gained strength that my parents never had. So in a strange way, I find I am not only grateful that I survived my childhood, but I am grateful FOR my childhood. Without my wounded youth, I might have become more complacent, less intensely involved with and appreciative of the miracle of raising a child. Being a part of my daughter's life has helped me to become reconciled to my past, grateful for the present, and hopeful about the future.

THE EASTER EGG HUNT

I took my daughter to an Easter egg hunt. We didn't find any eggs. My daughter was searching and searching and muttering, "I knew we wouldn't find any! I knew we wouldn't find any!" I took a piece of candy and hid it and helped her find it. She recognized it as something I had put in her basket at a party before we went to the hunt. There was nothing I could do to fix it for her. She was sad. I was sad. We both had a lousy time. I talked to her on the way home about you-can't-always-get-what-you-want, la-dee-da-dee-da.

The next morning at the breakfast table while my daughter was still asleep, I began to weep. My daughter was disappointed, as any four-year-old would be, and she judged the whole affair a failure because she didn't find an egg. I cried because I identified with her so much. As a child I was always hunting everywhere everywhere everywhere for the egg (love) and never finding it. So the feelings from my past came up over an Easter egg hunt. I have spent my life hunting down love, scouring the earth for that brightly colored orb of life. But I keep turning up leaves and twigs. Sometimes I think I have found one, but it turns out to be a stone. Maybe I've been looking in all the wrong places.

We had another Easter egg hunt. This one I set up. My daughter found lots of love. And fun. And the Easter eggs weren't bad either.

STANDING UP FOR MYSELF

My daughter had a play date with her friend. I took them to a children's theatre. The other child is a year older than my daughter and she is a little more devious and sophisticated. At one point this little girl picked up two pieces of paper, both of which were clearly the same size, and she claimed one was much larger than the other. She proceeded to offer the "smaller" one to my daughter, who began to cry and to ask me why she couldn't have the "bigger" one.

I tried to explain to her that the two pieces of paper were the same size and that her friend was playing a trick on her. I told her that the size difference was all in her mind. I suggested that she go up to her friend and tell her that her piece of paper was not bigger. I told her that if she would stand up for herself she would see that the other little girl only had as much power over has as she was willing to give her. My daughter just stood there crying and asking for the larger piece of paper.

I became furious with her for not standing up for herself. Then I felt guilty for not standing up for my daughter because she could not stand up for herself. I felt further guilt when I realized I was asking a four-year-old to stand up for herself in a way that I am barely able to do as a thirty-five-year-old man. I felt guilty about the fact that I was very disappointed and angry with my little girl.

I remember that when I was a child I literally could not stand up for myself. I was a cripple. I did not learn to walk until I was seven. My father and mother were cripples also. But they were spiritually crippled. I leaned on my crutches. My father leaned on the bottle. My mother leaned on my father. None of us could or would stand up for ourselves. As a young man, I became an alcoholic and a drug addict. I never held a steady job until I was over thirty years old. I did whatever women told me to do. There were a million examples of how I couldn't stand up for myself. And if a woman came up to me now, tore this page out of my typewriter, held it up to another piece of typing paper, and told me one was bigger, I would probably believe her. If she held ME up next to her and told me she was better, I would probably believe her.

It is inappropriate for me to ask my daughter to resolve my self-esteem problems for me. It is especially inappropriate because she is four years old, but it would still be inappropriate if she were forty.

I feel grateful that, because I am trying to recover from the abuse of my youth, I am able to see these unresolved issues playing themselves out. Then I can accept the fact that there are a lot of unfortunate aspects of my character that need to be changed if I am to live a contented life. Then and only then do I become willing to let the change take place. It is amazing how many missing pieces of my puzzle are coming to me through my four-year-old daughter. Children are great teachers.

PANIC IN CENTRAL PARK

A herd of people
smiles on manic faces
chapped palmed hands
gesturing wildly
tongues wagging
voices competing.

My daughter panics
falls to all fours
cries and crawls
on black pavement
studded with pebbles.
Bits of green
broken glass
embedded in her skin.
Round spots of blood
in the shape of her knees
trail her.

I pick her up
brush the pain
off of her
but the panic remains.
She doesn't recognize me.
Love is no consolation.

A likeness of her father
scared by people
she runs away
damaging herself
in the process.
Scared too
by those she runs to
she wants to break away
from even
her rescuer.

Someday perhaps...

To my darling daughter Celeste who is with her mother's relatives in a large farm house in Connecticut celebrating Thanksgiving.

God bless you, Celeste. Enjoy your day. Bask in the attention that your loved ones give to you today. I cannot give you a sense of family. But I want you to experience family. So I release you to your mother's family this holiday.

Enjoy the sensation of people caring for you. People who watch you so that you don't wander too close to the basement stairs. People who watch that you don't eat too much soda and candy. People who think of you before you arrive and bring out toys they know you will like. People who lovingly mediate your arguments with other children. People who cut your food for you, tuck a napkin into your shirt collar, and kiss you on the head.

I wish I had a family that you could feel a part of, Celeste. I am sorry for you and sorry for me that I don't. I will be with friends who love me today. I will be in good hands. I just want you to know that I am thinking of you. I love you. Happy Thanksgiving.

THE BLACK TIGHTS

The phone rang early in the morning. I knew who it had to be.

"You have our daughter's black tights and she can't go to ballet class without them," she said.

"Well, what are you going to do about it?" I asked, mustering all the self-assurance I don't have, repeating over and over to myself my mantra du jour: this is her problem, not mine.

"I don't know," she flatly replied, leaving unmentioned the supposed truth in our relationship that it is my duty to act and hers to react. She said good-bye and hung up.

I became furious. She knows that my personality dictates that I must do do do do do something about the black tights. And she has set it all up simply by calling me, and by leaving all the right things left unsaid, and by playing the pauses in the conversation with the skill of a master orator. She has set me up to assume the problem. And yet she hasn't asked me for a thing. She hasn't made a suggestion of what to do either. She hasn't made a commitment or an accusation. She has taken herself off the hook and allowed me to impale myself on it. She has taken her problem and handed it to me and I instinctively reached for it. I was furious at myself because I felt powerless over my need to take on her problems. And I was furious at her for letting me do it.

I went back into my bedroom and resumed my exercises with a vengeance. My daughter is with my former wife today, I said, as I punched an invisible punching bag, and she needs a piece of clothing. So why is that my problem? It was not nice of my wife to thrust her problems at me, but the real issue now is: why am I so willing to take them on? She has probably forgotten about the black tights knowing that I am suffering and agonizing and scheming and planning and into my head popped this sentence, "I have to get those black tights to her or I'll die!!!"

I tried to clear my head of that phantom thought by doing some pushups, but in my mind's eye all I could see was a room full of four-year-old girls wearing white tutus and black tights. Amidst them was one little girl who looks just like me standing in a corner with her white, bare, bird-like legs sticking out from under a tutu. I saw her refusing to participate in the class because she felt different than all the other girls.

That is how I felt my entire life as a child. I was a cripple and was physically kept apart from other children. My parents were alcoholics and I had to keep that a secret from my friends and I was sure no one else had that problem, no one else felt as isolated as I did. And when I saw the possibility that my daughter would feel a similar isolation, I became desperate to keep her from having to go through the same horror.

I understood a little better why I had taken on my wife's problem. It was because the real problem was me. And although I did not like the prospect of rescuing my former wife from her problem once again, I decided that, for the sake of easing my discomfort and for the sake of my daughter, I would call my former wife and offer to pay for a taxi to come to my house to pick up the tights and then take another taxi to the class at Carnegie Hall. When I called she told me she had found another pair of black tights and had forgotten to tell me. But she thanked me for the offer anyway.

PARTY BY DWIGHT

Every year for the last four I have thrown a birthday party for Celeste at the Manhattan restaurant where I work. It is elaborate beyond what I could afford if I did not work there.

Due to the generosity of my boss, I get a great price on all the food. There are eight hundred dollars worth of flowers all around. I arrange games, make sandwiches for the kids and crudites, fruit, cheeses, and beverages for the adults. After the party, when the guests are full of the special cake our pastry chef, Kurt, has made for Celeste, I take everyone on a horse-drawn carriage ride through Central Park.

And every year, without fail, several of the mothers (men don't attend these things) walk up to my former wife and thank her for the wonderful party.

Sexism works both ways. And it hurts. Some men don't consider women to be emotionally or physically equipped for some jobs. Some women don't consider men capable or willing to do other types of jobs. I hate to see my work ignored. It is the same feeling I have when I am the only—or one of the few—men in an aerobics class, and the instructor, in a fit of inspiration and perspiration, yells, "Come on, girls!!" An unintentional slip, yes. But it reinforces the stereotype that this is one of the things men don't do.

It is not only children and women who want to be appreciated and loved. I realize it is not the responsibility of children and women to make it easy for me to step out of my stereotypical male role into something more comfortable. It is my job to confront the labels and the limits some people, consciously or unconsciously, try to place on me.

The important thing is that my daughter had fun. The party was for her. It was not about me. But my feelings are real. I don't need to lose my identity in the process of meeting my daughter's needs.

Next year I might hang a banner in front of the restaurant which says, "Party by Dwight without the Help of Women If You Can Believe That."

Or I might even walk up to the persons thanking my former wife and offer to freshen their drinks and inform them gently that I am the host. I can take command of the situation. I can get comfortable in my new role. I can stop running around like a busboy who was built to serve and please women.

I can hire some people to do the busy work for me so I too can stroll around the party. It's nice to have choices, to have a voice that speaks up in my behalf. It's nice to see I am behaving like my own ally. I'm beginning to ask for what I need. I'm beginning to claim what is rightfully mine.

A SMALL PRICE TO PAY

My daughter woke up in the middle of the night
and ran toward the bathroom. She didn't make it.
She left a trail of pee from one end of the
apartment to the other. I cleaned up the mess
and was pleasantly surprised at how my
daughter seemed to feel absolutely no guilt
or embarrassment.

I remember when I was a child and my dog peed
on the carpet so my father shot him.
If I'd had an accident like my daughter's
I wonder if my father would have shot me?
It wasn't even safe to pee in my house.
I never knew if someone would walk into
the bathroom when I was sitting on the toilet.
None of us even lifted a fork without looking
out the corners of our eyes first.
Every offense was potentially punishable by
death.

Now I am an adult and I am afraid to move.
If I put a stamp upside down on an envelope
someone might shoot me.
I thought there was safety in immobility.
Someone said, "What do you want to be when
you grow up?" And I said, "A cactus." Alone
in a desert. Not even needing water. With plenty
of thorns.

. . • . .

But now I want more. I don't want to teach
my daughter how to isolate herself. I don't want her
to grow up thinking that the only thing worth
keeping is a pocket full of memories.
I want to move, but my fears have grown into
the soil and keep me standing here.
My fingers are groping through the quicksand
searching for the key I dropped there a lifetime ago.

Hope is bubbling in my veins and it is painful.
The fear of doing nothing is becoming
greater than the fear of reaching for my dreams.
My disease tells me I am not entitled to dreams
because my father was not entitled to his
and I must keep up the family tradition of
not deserving a decent life.

Fear is becoming a small price to pay for
becoming the person I want to be. I am not
recovering gracefully, but I am recovering.
My fear and I are becoming friends. I am
learning to become afraid of things I should
be afraid of. I walk on, despite the phantom
fear that I will be punished for being myself.

A BEAUTIFUL DAY TO TORMENT A CHILD

Sundays have always been rough for me, especially since my marriage broke up three years ago. Sundays have always felt like family days and I don't have a family, even though I long for one. So there is an edge, a sadness, a loneliness that is triggered in me every seventh day. The depth of my neediness sometimes makes me feel desperate for someone to talk to, to walk with, to care for and be cared for by.

It was what the weather reports referred to as "unseasonably warm," so my five-year-old daughter and I went into Central Park to celebrate the spring in winter. We paused near the Alice in Wonderland statue to listen to an obese, Charlie Chaplinesque violinist play "The Rites of Spring."

I got up my courage and sat down next to a young, attractive woman whom I had been watching while she watched the violinist. I can barely remember what she looked like, except that the color of her eyes matched the color of the water in the reflecting pool she sat next to. Oh, yes! I remember the sun glistening on her red, full lips. I almost forgot about her auburn hair, thick, shiny, and freshly cut. And her hands, long and thin with one broken nail. And her arms, cradled around her knees, which were pulled against her chest. She had a graceful, calm energy about her.

We began to talk about—what else?—the weather. Then we talked about the characters—the violinist included—who returned year after year to Central Park. We began to talk faster as our excitement for each other grew. At least that is the way it felt to me. Who knows what she was feeling? I was about to find out, though, when suddenly I heard, "Daddy. I want to go. Daddy!

Let's go!" At first my heart began to sink. I wondered if I could get away with pretending not to have heard it. No way. I began to panic. I think I would have rather heard from the Grim Reaper. I tried to dissuade her once or twice. But it became obvious that she was not going to ease up. I thought about asking this woman for her telephone number, but it was just too soon. Maybe if I had five more minutes to talk to her it would have seemed appropriate. Maybe. Maybe. Maybe. Celeste moaned and pouted and pulled on my heartstrings once more. I turned and said to Ms. Nearmiss, "Good-bye. Nice talking to you." Celeste and I abruptly departed for some damn playground.

I was hurt and angry at being pulled away from that young apparition, that thin connection to the human race, that rare hope of being cared for by someone. I became furious with Celeste, although at the time I didn't know it. I blamed God—although at the time I didn't know that either—for sending me a lovely woman for thirty seconds so I could leave the park even more lonely and frustrated than when I arrived. For the rest of the day, I thought I might run into her once more. I rehearsed my lines for the time when we would meet again. But, a little further within me, I realized that this is New York and you take an opportunity the instant it comes along or lose it forever.

I found myself being mean to Celeste. Sometimes I was overtly mean to her, saying things like, "Get over here right now or you're going to get it on the fanny," in response to some minor transgression. Sometimes I was passively mean to her—withholding love, being cold and quiet, walking nine steps in front of her, wishing I was alone and knowing she could pick up on that.

After being emotionally distant from her for about two hours we sat down to share an apple juice. We had left the park on that glorious first day of spring and Celeste was saying, "I don't ever ever ever want to go back there again." We were on the steps of the Frick Museum and I said, "There is something I want to talk to you about."

"I know what it is," she said.

"You do?" I asked, at once curious and apprehensive about her answer.

"You want to talk about what you did in the park," she said.

"What did I do in the park?"

"You hurt my feelings," she sobbed, holding back a gargantuan cry.

At that convenient moment she spilled the apple juice and we walked to the store to get another. When we returned to the museum steps we both were in a lighter mood. I could tell communication was now possible. Although my daughter is only five and a half, I decided to risk being honest about what was going on in me.

I told her that I recently had a series of disappointments. Publication of my book had been put on hold. I was upset with my parents. I told her I was angry with her mother and I explained the situation a little bit. I told her I had a lot of problems that had not been resolved yet. I let her in on my life without immersing her in conversation she was not able to comprehend. I told her one more problem of mine.

"I'm lonely," I said.

"But I'm here with you," she said in a tone so sincere and loving I almost collapsed on the pavement.

"And I'm very, very grateful for that," I said. "But you know when you are around adults all the time and you sometimes get lonely for the company of another child?"

"Uh-huh," she nodded, eager to understand.

"Well, I'm lonely for the company of another adult," I said.

I was unsure at this point whether I was being inappropriate in including Celeste in some of the issues behind my behavior. I felt strange talking to my daughter about intimacy issues concerning myself and a woman. It reminded me of when I was a child and my mother would speak to me like I was her shrink or her best friend. It made me feel that she was out of control and therefore I was in danger. But this felt different. There was an expression of recognition and empathy on Celeste's face. My mother was out of control; I am not. "I was very happy when I met that woman by the Alice in Wonderland statue," I continued. "And I wanted to be her friend. But you got upset and insisted that we leave. That made me a little sad and angry. Don't you want me to be her friend?"

"I don't mind if you're her friend," she replied.

"Then why were you so upset?" I asked.

"Because you weren't talking to me."

"Next time I will be sure to include you in the conversation," I said.

Celeste felt abandoned by me when I turned my attention to the new acquaintance. It wasn't that she absolutely did not want me to connect with another person. The issue was that she didn't want me to leave her in order to do so. It was a matter of me including her in my life when I am with her. Had I allowed my daughter to talk to the woman as well, things might have been different. But then again, they might not have. Chance encounters are merely chance encounters. Brief conversations in the park do not always lead to romance, thank God.

Perhaps a more accurate title for this piece would be "A Beautiful Day to Torment Myself." Have you noticed how I manage to blame myself for things not going the way I think they should? My daughter pulls me away from someone I'm talking to and somehow I manage to make it all my fault. I am a blame-collector. Every interaction between me and another person that doesn't work out is because of something I said or did. Only when everything is right can I absolve myself of blame for it being wrong.

I often consider it my responsibility to "fix" my daughter so that she will never feel uncomfortable. I think this stems from some residual guilt about my wife and I splitting up. In some ways I feel that one way of making it up to Celeste for her broken home is to provide her with my undivided attention. I dote on my daughter. I rarely date women. Sometimes I feel as if I am remaining loyal to a family that no longer exists. I feel guilty that I'm not perfect. I feel angry that my best wasn't good enough. I feel bad that my best attempts to guarantee that Celeste would have two parents who stayed together failed. So I have tried to be everything and everybody for her. What an awesome responsibility! I have become exhausted and frustrated and lonely. Celeste never asked me to do this. She only asked me to stay with her in the park.

I did not have a problem with my daughter that day. I had a problem with myself. My daughter split me apart from the competition. I let her do it. Such was my need to keep peace with my daughter. The name of my game is "Peace at Any Price"! But it backfired. I walked away from the possibility of having the female companionship I needed. Celeste wanted her Daddy all to herself. And she got him. What I got for going along with it was fury. I voluntarily subjugated my needs to Celeste's. That has been my lifelong role with everyone. "You First" is the name of my second favorite game. I play that game with lovers and bosses and family and friends. No matter who the person is, the lesson remains the same.

I must take care of myself first. Celeste and I were on a plane recently. The flight attendant was going through her pre-takeoff spiel. I listened very closely as she explained the use of emergency oxygen. "If you are traveling with a small child, place the oxygen mask over your face FIRST so that you may better assist the child."

How simple. How logical. If I am suffocating myself because I am not tending to my own needs, how can I ever expect to give appropriate assistance to another person?

I will take Celeste's advice and include her in conversations I am having with other people, so as to make her feel comfortable and not left out. I know what it's like to be a child and feel left out. But the next time I am in a situation like that, I will probably inform Celeste that I am busy talking to someone and I intend to continue doing so. I will explain that when the conversation is over I will take her to the playground. That way we both get a chance. There is plenty of life for everyone. I can't wait for anyone, especially a child, to give me permission to take my share, to live my life as I see fit. I will respect myself for that and, although Celeste may still want me all to herself, she will benefit from seeing her father treat himself with benevolent self-respect.

It sure is too bad that life's lessons, those beautiful gifts, are so often wrapped in pain. But how else would I get myself to sit down and think it through and find out what is behind my failures and disappointments, so that I may learn how to change and become more comfortable as a person and a parent? Sometimes gifts come in strange packages. I am sorry the woman in the park is gone. It would have been fun to get to know her. But without failing to connect with her, I wouldn't have had the opportunity to learn all this. She was a great teacher.

LITTLE GIRL LOST
LITTLE BOY FOUND

I couldn't find my little girl. Perhaps she wasn't supposed to be with me that day. Prone to hysteria anyway, I decided not to worry about it. Take a positive outlook. She is probably with her mother, I told myself. I went to sleep that night feeling—uh—proud of myself. I'm breaking the habit of negative projection. She is with her mother. I think. Umm...pretty sure.

Next morning, a few hours after I woke, I called her mother. "Celeste disappeared in a crowd yesterday. Have you seen her?" I could feel the panic in my throat. Until I felt the words in my mouth I had completely convinced myself that Celeste was all right. I knew better now. Celeste was gone.

"What do you mean she disappeared? No she's not with me! Where is my daughter?"

I resented her speaking to me in that harsh tone.

Again, I felt the panic bubbling in my throat. I could feel it spread through my veins. I decided not to give in. I would not succumb to the pain and loss and fear and dread. I'd had enough of that in my life already. Besides, why waste the emotion? Celeste will be back. She's probably out on a long walk. So what if she's only five. She's very mature for her age.

I crawled into bed with my clothes still on and pulled the sheets over my head. I fell asleep.

· · • · ·

I woke up. What a horrid dream! Losing my daughter and not being able to feel it. I remember that before I went to sleep I was thinking how tired I am of being a responsible parent. I want to be an irresponsible child sometimes. I want to get mud on my clothes. I want to eat ice cream then popcorn then ice cream again. I want to get on a bus and ride it until I arrive back at the point where I got on. I want to go to a lousy movie. I want to crank the stereo up and dance naked.

So in my dream I lose my daughter on the streets of New York in order to avoid feeling that I am drowning in a sea of responsibility. I mistake responsibility for seriousness. I have become very serious about my seriousness.

I want to play. I want to play. I want to play. Damn it. I want to play—before I have to discard everyone and break everything which my dreams tell me stand between me and freedom.

The little boy in me is getting restless. Feels left out. Sibling rivalry. I give all my attention to my daughter and none to the child within me. I don't want to have to lose my daughter in order to find myself. My daughter led me to the child within me and pointed to a little boy sitting in that dark corner all alone. I will make the introduction. I will give the little boy permission to come out and play with my daughter.

INTERNAL SIBLING RIVALRY

He puts his child on the carousel
but the child within him
must wait by the gate.

>He buys his child an ice cream
>but the child within him
>must watch his calories.

His child skips and sings a spring song
but the child within him
sits still and is silent.

>He puts his child to bed on time
>but the child within him
>must lie awake, thinking.

The child within him
resents the child outside of him.
"Why do you get to have all the fun?"

>Perhaps the child within him
>can come out and play
>with his daughter.
>
>A truce can be declared,
>a friendship risked.
>One child can teach the other
>about darkness.
>The other can teach the other
>about light.
>
>There is enough love
>to go around
>and in
>and through
>me and you.

LESSONS ON A CAROUSEL

What a great idea! I will take my daughter with me to a national convention of adult children of alcoholics meeting near Disney World! They have child care available. Who could be more sensitive to the needs of my daughter than a group of adults who were poorly raised?

We had a great time. I took Celeste to her first dance (she is only five-and-a-half). She loved the loud music and the flashing lights. She saw adults kick off their shoes and have fun. "Adults need to play too," I said to her. I carried her in my arms onto the dance floor and danced one fast and one slow song with her before it was her bedtime.

The next day I put Celeste on a carousel located in the middle of the convention hall. I stood watching her with a grin on my face, a perfect picture of a proud parent. I took her to the games on Carnival Night and watched her win all sorts of stuffed toys. I took her to Disney World and Epcot Center. She loved it! I put her back on the carousel and as I was watching her go around and around my mind and heart stopped in unison, "Hey! Wait a

minute!" I said to myself, "Why haven't I played any of these games? These games were set up for adult children as well as for young children. The child in me wants to come out and play."

I realized that the convention was set up for the child in me more so than for my child. I had placed myself in an adult, parent role and was ignoring the child in me who wanted to come out and play and discuss problems with other adult children. Every night I was in bed early, planning the next wonderful excursion for Celeste. But I was also thinking of the other adults, sitting in each other's rooms, laughing, talking, staying up too late. I longed for that. One evening someone said to me, "Seeing you here with your beautiful daughter is a very moving sight. But I feel for you, having to take care of your daughter and not being able to be here for yourself." I resented that statement very much, as I often do when someone tells me something I suspect is true but don't want to hear. I went back to our hotel room and prepared Celeste for bed.

As she was about to get into bed, she said to me, "Where is my doggie?"

"What do you mean?" I asked.

"This morning I had four stuffed animals on my bed. Now there are three. Where is my doggie?" She began to cry. I went into the bathroom and shut the door. I began to cry too. The child within me was very saddened by the loss of my daughter's doggie. But the parent in me didn't feel safe to show it. So I cried with my face in a towel, as I have done several times before, and I emerged from the bathroom stoic and in control a few minutes later.

I called housekeeping to see if the doggie had been rolled up in the bedsheets. No luck. A few minutes later hotel security arrived at our room to investigate the "crime." He was dressed like a cop, and Celeste was quite impressed that I had called the police to help locate her stuffed doggie.

"Did you let anyone into the room?" the officer wanted to know.

"No one was here who could have stolen the brown doggie with the long, black ears, officer," I replied, concealing a laugh at the ridiculousness of the conversation.

We never did find the doggie. I think Celeste has forgotten about it. Obviously I haven't.

The next day I was wearing thin. I had, innocently enough, scheduled myself so that I couldn't get away from Celeste to take care of my own emotional needs. Children are not big on gratitude.
I thought that since she saw me giving 150 percent to her, she would take it easy on me and let me recuperate the next day. Not so. She was now ready to shoot for 175 percent.

We returned to New York, and I took Celeste to spend half of the week with her mother, as is our custodial arrangement. I went home and collapsed in a sea of emptiness. I had abandoned myself so as to be there for Celeste.

I realize now that this is a question of balance. I must learn how to take care of my daughter without being swamped by her needs. For the first two years that we lived alone together I wouldn't even date women. I wouldn't hire a babysitter. I wouldn't read a book while she was here. I was a Macho Dad who didn't need anyone. I could sew and cook and scold and braid hair and earn a decent living and pamper and nurture with the best of them. And I was damned sure that my daughter wouldn't suffer from neglect that way I did as a child. The problem was I was suffering from neglecting myself as an adult. I felt the bitterness and self-pity

creeping in at the convention. It is time to change that.
Celeste is not ecstatic that I no longer kowtow to her every whim. Neither am I. It feels weird to say no to Celeste so that I can say yes to myself. Celeste wants to have a play date with a friend and her mother tomorrow. I thought it over and I will not do it. I feel very uncomfortable around the child's mother. My old way of doing things would be to swallow my discomfort so that Celeste could have fun. I can't get away with that way of thinking anymore. My recovery won't let me. Perhaps a compromise might be reached. I might ask the mother if I can take both kids for the afternoon and that way the mother can have the day to herself.

I understand and forgive myself for tipping the scales in the opposite direction of the way my parents raised me. I know a child's pain, and I sometimes overcompensate so that she doesn't have to go through what I did. But she never will go through what I did. She has different parents, and she is a different person. The more whole I become, the better parent I will be.

I now ride the carousel in Central Park with Celeste. There has always been a seat there for the child within me. All it takes is to see it. And the courage to go for a ride.

THE PROP

I took my daughter to see New York's best mime artist perform. He selected me from the audience to assist him in a skit. I was totally horrified! He cut through my cloak of invisibility, which I use to hide myself from the world, and pulled me by the hand up onto the stage. I was very surprised that he selected me. Until that day I could not imagine anyone choosing me to share the stage with. I had always emitted extremely strong messages of "stay the hell away from me! I'm angry and one thing you don't want to do is to mess with me!" I figured my aura of rage must be diminishing in order for the performer to choose me to assist him, knowing that, in part, his act balanced on how successful he was in choosing the right person from the audience.

When I was on the stage, he stiffened his body and began to fall toward me. He would have hit the floor had I not caught him. He trusted me to get into the act. His body was dead weight. It took all the strength I had to push him back into an upright position and as soon as I did he fell forward again. I felt like Sisyphus, rolling him back into a standing position only to have him fall toward me time and time again. The audience loved it.

I didn't. I did not enjoy the feeling of being a prop in someone's act. It reminded me of the feelings I had as a child in an alcoholic home. It seemed they were always falling over, collapsing under the weight of their drunkenness or their failure. They always seemed to fall toward me and I had to be the one to prop them up. Why didn't they ever fall toward each other? I felt like a prop which they needed to act out their drama. I felt like a prop they used to blame each other for their failures.

They were always saying, "Look what you've done to Dwight. Look how you've made him feel." But it was never with any regard for me. It was always just a way of jabbing at each other. Sometimes they would play a game called "Hot Potato" with me. I got to be the potato and they tossed me back and forth as quickly as possible, for they both knew I was too hot to handle.

Sometimes I had no apparent role. I would adorn their set like a piece of furniture, which was never used but was there because it made the place look somehow complete. Sometimes I was the "fall guy" and they would speak to each other through me. Sometimes my job was just to be there like a pillar in the center of the room for them to lean on.

One day I sewed myself a cloak of invisibility. I put it on and never took it off. Never. Not for one moment. I felt that if I would stand offstage and not move or make a sound or breathe, I would be left alone. And alone I was. And invisible I was—to the point where I began to wonder if I existed. I had heard the slogan "Out of sight, out of mind." I was out of their sight. And I felt like I was going out of my mind.

But there I was on stage again for the first time in years. I was once again a prop. And yet it was funny, and it was harmless, and it was kind. I felt a part of the humor but not the brunt of the joke.

I looked out into the audience and saw my daughter watching me. She could tell I was red-faced and embarrassed. She knew it was difficult for me to be up there. But I did it anyway, and it was good for her to see her father take a risk. I was not one of those parents who pushed their kids toward the stage saying, "Go on up there! Go on up there! What are you afraid of?" when if they had to do it themselves they'd be scared to death. I participated. I had fun. I was rewarded with applause. The audience was sometimes laughing with me and sometimes laughing at me, and both situations were all right.

I allowed my cloak of invisibility to be taken from my shoulders by a mime artist in New York City. I felt fine without it. The season had changed and I didn't need it anymore. I had thought the cloak kept me in. But what it really did was to keep the world out.

The fabric my cloak had been made of was self-consciousness. I was so wrapped up in myself that I couldn't see anything and therefore thought I was invisible. I had only succeeded in keeping myself hidden from myself.

I have allowed more and more people to see me since that day. Many like what they see. And I have allowed myself to see more and more of myself since that day. And I like what I see.

I see myself coming out of myself and moving into the world. I allow myself to interact with people as a man among men, a person among people. I am not a walking secret anymore. I am an open book. And good reading too!

DOING IT BACKWARDS IS RIGHT

I was doing some exercises on the living room floor. Celeste was sitting on the couch, drawing. "I made a book," she said, "and I am going to put the telephone numbers of all my friends in it. Go get your address book and read the numbers to me and I will copy them into my book." When she was finished she proudly handed the book to me. One of the phone numbers I saw looked like this:

I complimented her on her work and said to her, "I have to tell you that two of the numbers are backwards."

"They are not," she said.

"I must be honest with you and tell you that they are."

"I have the right to write them the way I want to."

"Yes you do. And I have the right to tell you that they are backwards." She became extremely frustrated and put the book away.

Later that morning I told her teacher what had happened and how I had corrected her, and he said, "Don't do it. By writing the numbers she is working a little beyond her ability as it is. One day she will look at the page and say to herself 'this number is backward' and she will correct it. The potential harm lies in her deciding not to do the work because it doesn't please you."

What Celeste had wanted by showing the book to me was validation for her efforts. She wanted to be appreciated and encouraged for her efforts to reach a little beyond her ability to learn something new. Her self-respect and her confidence were the real issues here, much more so than learning how to master the writing of numbers.

My reaction to learning this was interesting: it made me sick to my stomach. I felt as if I had damaged her terribly by trying to correct her. Gradually, I gained a healthier perspective of the situation. I congratulated myself on perceiving the possible error so quickly. The problem came up, and one hour later I had already discussed it with her teacher. Yet the throb in my stomach persisted. I allowed myself a couple of hours to get into the feeling.

As a child I was always being corrected. The object of the correction was to make me as much like my parents as possible. Yet they were sick people, and their beliefs and behavior and attitudes vacillated tremendously from day to day, sometimes hour to hour. I was trained to spell something the way they spelled it, whether that was the way it appeared in the dictionary or not. There was no time to relax and be myself. There was no time to experiment with different ways of doing things. There was one way to put on a shirt, to answer a phone, to speak to my mother, to do the dishes, to say goodnight. There was one way to think, and that was to think just like Dad. Anything else was treason. I became very rigid in my thinking. Experimentation was heresy. Dogma was divine. Mistakes were openly ridiculed.

Now I am an adult and I am saying that it is fine that my daughter writes her numbers backwards. Life is weird. This task of dismantling my life is amazing. I am writing my life backwards. I am trying to be open and flexible, to realize that my daughter knows more about being a child than I do. In a strange way I am asking her to help me be her parent. And she is. I don't need all this control. My daughter and I are growing up together. It isn't as difficult as I thought it would be. Asking for help helps.

NOT GOING TO CAPE COD

My "X" and her boyfriend picked up my daughter, Celeste, to take her to Cape Cod for three weeks. They walked out of the door, and I sat down at the breakfast table to have a cup of coffee. Lying on the table was a barrette I use to keep the hair out of Celeste's eyes. I looked at that white, plastic thing—a symbol of all she is and means to me—and I began to cry.

This is why I try not to love. I feel so vulnerable. If something happened to my daughter, I really don't think I could survive. I wonder if there are people who don't think like this? Are they the numb ones? The dumb ones? The healthy ones? Is trying not to love a sound idea?

I am used to losing or not getting what I love. I often feel that the other shoe has already dropped. I am just waiting for the sound to reach my ears.

Before Celeste left this morning, she began to cry and confided in me that she was afraid she was going to die in a car accident on the way to the Cape. Since I am as much a child as she is, I began (secretly) to worry about a car accident also. Is she psychic like me? Can she see the future? Is she merely negative and slightly paranoid like me? Can she only see the underside of the future? Is she just being a little girl expressing, in her own way, the primal fear that if she ventures out into the unknown without her Daddy she will die?

No matter. I thought it best to take an action. "Shall we say a prayer for you?" I asked.

"Yes," she said, matter-of-factly.

"Would you like to join me?" I asked.

"No," she said, "I would like to watch."

She heard me end my prayer with, "Thy will be done." She wanted to know what I would think if God decided he wanted her dead. I told her I had faith in God's decisions. That answer did not please her. I quickly added that I thought we would both lead a long life. I told her I thought God had a plan for us here on earth. "I feel God needs us here to do His work," I said. I asked her if she felt better and she said, "Kind of."

Her mother arrived. Her boyfriend stayed in the car out front, with the motor running, tapping his fingernails on the steering wheel. Her mother stood by the kitchen sink as I combed Celeste's hair, put her moccasins on, gave her some orange juice, and brushed her teeth. I reminded her that I had said a prayer for her safety. I told her mother about her fear and asked her to drive carefully. I told her there was not much else I could do. I gave her a hug and whispered in her ear as I have so many, many times before, "I am your one and only Daddy. I am here to love you forever. No matter what. No matter when. I am here to love you forever."

I continued to play with the white, plastic barrette. I began to cry some more. My adult self cried because I missed my daughter. I am not used to her being gone. The child within me cried because I was left behind again.

Everyone is going to the beach except me! I am going to my mind. To my fantasies. To the land where no one leaves. But there is no beach there. Once again I have not protected myself by having a beach for ME to go to. I always set it up so that I feel that there is not enough fun to go around. The world has just enough cake minus one slice.

But I am getting better at this. I can see how I set myself up for pain by not having something fun for me to do today. But I have arranged for some gigantic fun for the three weeks ahead. In the meantime I am going to take care of today. I am going to get up off of my butt and make a few phone calls, check out the museums and movies. I live in the middle of New York City and there is lots to do here.

My daughter left and my first reaction was to feel immobilized by pain again. That is my old, very familiar way of doing things. But then my adult self took the child within me by the hand and walked him to this table where I write this. Here I am free to feel the emotions that came up when my daughter left. Here I realize that it is not so much her leaving but my being left behind that bothers me. Here I choose to focus on the prayer and faith and courage and positivity that I spoke to Celeste about. Here I choose to absorb some of my own message.

I believe that things will work out just fine until proved otherwise. I believe that this three-week separation will be good for Celeste and for me. I do not have to feel guilty that part of me is glad to be away from the responsibility of parenting for a while. I am glad for this additional lesson in letting go. I'm glad for this lesson that, even though I am the father of a five-year-old girl, I must still be my first priority. Eventually, all leave—except God.

Guess what? There is enough cake for everyone! There are no missing pieces. There is enough life to go around! Have a happy summer!

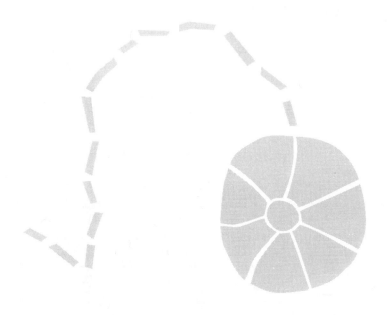

OUR HAMSTER PREFERS...

...small spaces. I bought him for my daughter two Sundays ago. She wanted a dog. We live in a small Manhattan apartment and there isn't room for a dog. There barely is room for a hamster. But she deserves a pet, and I want her to learn about being responsible —although I will admit that, so far, I am the one who cleans the cage. I feared the worst and it has happened. I am the one who is learning to be more responsible at a time when the last thing I want is more responsibility.

The sales clerk at the pet store must prefer small spaces also. That's probably why he sold us a cage about the size of a hamster coffin. Maybe he was trying to be economical by selling us a home the hamster can be buried in. "Hold onto the receipt," he casually informed us. "There is a seven-day guarantee on the hamster."

My daughter looked at me and said, "What does that mean, Daddy?"

"It means they promise the hamster will be healthy and happy," I said to her. I felt responsible for the life of a rodent. The feeling of having to deal with a seven-year-old girl cupping a seven-day-old dead hamster in her hands and looking up at me and crying was not offset by the knowledge that I would get my $4.99 back.

We had no idea how small the cage was until we got home because the box was so BIG. It reminded me of one of those false-bottom yogurt cups; you are always stunned when you reach the bottom so quickly. Then you turn the cup over and discover it is standing on a half-inch-high circular stilt. The cage was definitely too small but it was already home and unpacked. We had an irate hamster screaming at us from within a lightless, cardboard box about the size of a Chinese food take-out container the sales clerk gave us to transport the hamster in.

We put the hamster inside the coffin-sized cage. He seemed to cope with it, but he slept a lot. That's a sign of boredom. Isn't it amazing how much knowledge on such a vast array of subjects you can accumulate by the time you become an adult? Just look, for example, at how much I know, without even trying, about boredom in rodents. I couldn't get back to the pet store to do something about the cage for a week, so every night I talked to the hamster in a voice laced with concern and a touch of guilt. I told him how we were going to get him out of there someday. I encouraged him to keep a stiff upper lip. I got claustrophobic just looking at our hamster in his very small space.

The week passed as quickly as a seven-day continuous math test. Eventually, it was Sunday again. My daughter and I went to church. The minister was out of town and his wife was sick so we offered to take their daughter for the day. Two kids are often more fun than one and, besides, if getting to heaven is based on a hundred-point system, taking the minister's daughter for a day is worth at least five.

We went back to the pet store and bought a HUGE hamster cage. The sales clerk informed me, while the children were off making faces at the goldfish, that a free hamster came with the new cage. I informed him that under no circumstances was he to tell the children that. The thought of not being able to get to sleep because of the sound of two hamsters chattering, chasing each other, or (yuk!) making love was not particularly appealing to me. I have no idea what sex our hamster is and I have no intention of doing what I would have to do to find out.

We got the new cage home and unboxed it. It was four times the size of the last one. It had everything in it but a tanning salon. We connected it to the old cage with a clear, yellow plastic tube about two feet long. I call it the subway. The kids and I worked very hard on it and there it was—ta-da!—a new home!

The hamster wanted nothing to do with his new cage. He stuffs wood chips into one end of the tube so he doesn't have to see or even think about the existence of the other house. The new addition just sits there like a boarded-up, abandoned, haunted hamster mansion. I tried to force him to like it. I put his food only in the large cage. He simply carried the food mouthful by mouthful into a corner of the smaller cage. I put a ferris wheel, fresh broccoli, and toys in the larger cage. I tried putting all the wood chips, which he used as bedding, in only the large cage. Nothing worked.

Our hamster prefers small spaces. Or is it that he can't handle large spaces? Is it because that first, crucial week at our house was spent in a small space that he is unable to feel comfortable anyplace else? Why does he deny himself access to a greater arena in which to live his life?

If I had a lot of money I would buy a mansion. Then I would probably move into one room of it. Maybe two. Perhaps three. Lately I have noticed how often I engage in small talk. I frequently am the possessor of small thoughts. I am the bearer of a sometimes small heart. I like small cars, small portions, small hotels, and small paychecks. (It is easier to rationalize a small world if you can't afford a larger one.)

All my clothes are too small. I look like a little boy growing out of his world. My shirtsleeves have never seen my wrists. I can't button the top button of my shirt without my head turning red. I never have to worry about getting my pant legs wet when I step in a puddle because they end a few inches above my shoes. Low ceilings are perfect for me. If I had lived in ancient Japan I would have had my feet bound. A straightjacket is my idea of pajamas.

I try to make my world small. My life is like an all-cotton shirt I throw into a hot clothes dryer. I shrink my world until I am about all that can fit in it.

I do this because I feel that if I make my world very small then it will be easier to control. Life will be more manageable. Things might get too close for comfort once in a while, but that is a small price to pay for being in control of my world.

It all began in my mother's womb, which I remember being very small. I didn't want to be born and have to live in such a large space. In small spaces I have a much better sense of boundaries. I know where things end and other things begin. I reach out to the horizons of the world and pull them in until they touch me. I wrap them around me like a blanket. Then I feel safe and warm.

· · ● · ·

I am changing. I live in a large world now. I made it large. I pray for the willingness to push on the walls of my world. The walls move back. The world is larger. I pray for the strength and courage to push again. The walls move further back. My world is larger still. I pray for the willingness to open doors, and to open the doors behind those doors. I pray for the strength to turn and walk away from the screaming demon who begs me to return to where I don't belong.

I deserve a larger world. I am more comfortable in a larger world. I no longer feel right in small clothes, small rooms, or small minds. I do not need to accept the limited vision of limited people. The world will not be a parent telling me to stay in my room. A small cage will not be my home.

Recovery means every day being less and less like a hamster. Our hamster prefers small spaces. I don't.

WITHOUT A TRACE

The little girl spilled her cola. Everyone froze. My daughter clutched her paper cup to her chest as if a friend spilling her cola were a contagious disease and she was afraid she would catch it.

The little girl, Cynthia, looked at me. My daughter, Celeste, looked at her. I looked at them both. It was a triangle of glances. Each waited for another one to move. Eventually mindful of my role as an adult, they both looked at me. "So what now?" their sweet little blank expressions said to me.

"The line in the snack bar is very long today. I don't want to go back in there. Maybe Celeste will share her cola with you," I said. Celeste clutched her cup even tighter and began a long, slow, confident, possessive suck on her straw. "On second thought," I said immediately, "Why don't you take my orange juice, Cynthia?"

Cynthia looked at me and then at Celeste. "I really don't need anything to drink," she said without a trace of insincerity. Her utter lack of manipulation, the fact that she hadn't tried to blame anyone for causing her to spill her drink, the fact that there was not even a hint of anger directed at her for having spilled the drink, the absolute acceptance of what had happened, the lack of pleading and whining—all of these things and more contributed to Celeste's and my desire to share what we had with her.

We walked up the big rock overlooking the flotilla of rowboats on Central Park Lake. I pulled out my secret stash of Zebra Cookies (a treat a friendly pastry chef makes and occasionally gives to Celeste). We had cookies and drinks in the early spring sun. The children put two straws in the one remaining paper cup of cola and took turns drinking. Once they drank from their straws at the same time and their foreheads almost touched like the fingertips reaching across the ceiling of the Sistine Chapel. They did not glue their eyes to the straw to measure the amount of cola flowing through it. Neither panicked at the possibility of the other child getting more.

They shared equally and lovingly, in the joy of the cool early spring breeze, the splendor of fresh-baked cookies, the slightly stinging bubbles of cold cola, and the unequaled warmth of childhood friendship.

MY DAUGHTER IS A COA, BUT LOOK!
Exerpts from Celeste's school report

"Celeste is a bright, friendly child who adjusted quickly and easily to school....

"When working alone, she often sits in close proximity to her friends so that she can carry on conversations. She also relates well with adults....

"When working alone, Celeste selects challenging materials and has a wide range of interests. Her observation skills are excellent. She is a highly-focused child who works in an unhurried manner and independently chooses and completes activities. She pays close attention to details, grasps concepts quickly, and applies them to the materials appropriately....

"Her curiosity and bright personality have been a delightful addition to our class....

"Celeste is a well-behaved, softspoken girl with a positive self-image. She takes pride in whatever she does. She is independent, well-coordinated and very aware of her own capabilities....

"Celeste is a serious, hard-working student who is always willing to try new, challenging activities. She has a long attention span.

"Celeste is an even-tempered, serious girl who, in the beginning of the year, strove to be 'perfect' in the class. She followed every rule to a 'T' and was extremely controlled. Lately she has been able to relax and 'let her hair down.' We are delighted to say that now there are times when she may need reminding of rules....

"She is even-tempered with great inner strength....

"A very friendly, verbal girl, she loved to start her day by chatting about her home experiences, which she always shared freely....

"She is very much loved and respected by her peers...."

ON BEING LOYAL

I thought that not getting involved with women
for two years was an expression of my desire to
become intimate with myself before jumping into
another crazy twisted love affair.

It wasn't that simple.

I thought that I was actually staying away
from women because of loyalty to my ex-wife.
Imagine that!

The startling realization of displaced loyalty
did not stop me from isolating myself and staying away
from women. Awareness was not enough to change
my behavior.

There must be some other reason.

One day in the shower, where I do my best thinking,
I realized it is not my ex-wife I am being loyal to.
It is my five-year-old daughter! By not allowing
myself a love, I am being faithful to my relationship
with my child.

Where did I learn that?

I am married to my daughter the way my mother
was married to me. My relationship with my mother
was supposed to be enough. I feel like an infidel
when I venture outside the family.

I am allowing women into my life now.

It feels like I am pulling away from my daughter.
I am. She is not my everything. I am not her
everyone. My distance from her is not far.
The space between us provides room to grow in.

I am being unfaithful to my ex-self.

I embrace my new life, which continues in an onward
and upward direction. What a relief not to live
with the disease of my family wrapped like gauze
around my heart!

PART FOUR

I SMELL FREEDOM

I SMELL FREEDOM

I survived against great odds. I am lucky to be here. I have met many people, including members of my family, who were raised in the way I was and, try as they may, they cannot piece together a decent life. Too much damage was inflicted for too long.

Many of us have worked very hard to become aware of and accept what happened to us as children, in hope that we might change for the better. But we can only work with the tools made available to us. A legless man may try hard to walk but the odds are not good. It is so uncanny that little groups of troubled people huddle together to talk about their childhoods and they get better. By virtue of what? We recover with lots of hard work and by the grace of a Power whose strength is greater than the group or any of the members in it. I have witnessed incredible progress in my friends where, by their own admission, they would have been incapable of it had they tried to do the work alone.

I have hope that I can recover. I have hope that with hard work, the help of friends, and the grace of a Power greater than myself, whom I choose to call God, I can begin to lead a normal life despite what I have been through and the damage it has caused. I took the lessons in negativity and despair I learned as a child and I embellished them as an adult. I accepted the negativity as if it were a fact, and I developed it as if it were an art. I live in a prison of my own making. I have hope that I can discover the origins of my troubles and accept responsibility for dealing with them. There is no one left to blame. The job of recovery belongs to me and my Higher Power.

I have hope that, because of recovery, I can raise my daughter differently than the way I was raised. I have hope that I can resurrect the child buried deep within me who went into hiding when the pain became too great. I hope I can coax him out and that he will believe me that it is safe to return to the world. I hope that I can walk the face of the earth as a man freed from the bondage of self. I hope that I can loosen up and have a good friendship with myself and treat myself with dignity and respect.

I hope that I will not continue to reach toward sick people and ask them to solve my life for me. I hope I can do my own homework. I hope that I can trust myself enough to let all my feelings surface, without fearing that there is some fatal feeling lurking in me that is just waiting to come out so that it can waste me. I hope I can learn that accepting a horrible feeling is not nearly as dangerous as stuffing one deep within me, only to have it fester and ooze its poison into every cell of my body. I hope I can realize that when I look in the mirror I am looking at the problem—as well as the solution. I hope I can stop asking women to play God and then being disappointed in their performance. I hope I can find my own voice. I hope I can learn to be myself, rather than a composite of what other people want me to be. I hope to be able to look at my past, let go of it, move on, and lighten up. Because I was willing to look at my past, I am able to be excited about my future. I smell freedom....

ADULT CHILDREN OF ALCOHOLICS

I was in recovery for several years when I noticed that many issues in my life simply had not budged. I was angry a lot but I couldn't trace the source of the anger. I had headaches. I had no friends in whom I felt safe to confide the secrets I was hiding from everyone including myself. My marriage was falling apart even though I was trying harder than ever to save it. We were unable to achieve intimacy in our marriage. There was a moat of distrust which separated us from a sense of partnership. I was uncomfortable around people. When I was alone I felt like I was in the presence of a hostile stranger. The world seemed to be an unsafe place populated by people who could not be trusted.

I knew something was wrong. I began to suspect that the secret to my unhappiness might be in my childhood. I was a cripple for five years when I was very young. I was raised in a foreign country by two violent, alcoholic parents in a military family. My childhood had been a nightmare.

I had the naive belief that all the scars would disappear simply by growing into adulthood. With time, many of my problems did disappear. But there were many residual effects from the early deprivation.

I remember arguing with my wife and in the middle of the argument I realized I couldn't care less about the issue. I was defending something my father cared very much about but which mattered very little to me. I found myself thinking, behaving, and even sounding exactly like my father. I was reenacting the way I had learned a man and woman are supposed to relate to each other. The problem was I had learned the behavior from two very sick role models.

My marriage fell apart and I found myself a single parent with joint custody of our daughter. I was without a wife and felt myself thrust into the role of being a "Mommydaddy" without benefit of having been successfully parented myself. In other words, I didn't know what I was doing. Thanks to a self-help group, books, and total devotion to my daughter, things have worked very well.

A year after separating from my wife I met a woman who began to love me. She and my daughter and I were in the playground one Sunday. I was feeling rather melancholic and my friend asked me what was the matter. I told her that Sundays always seemed like family days to me and that I didn't have a family and that made me feel very sad. She asked me what I thought a happy family might be doing on such a Sunday. I told her a family might play in the park, buy the paper, get an ice cream cone, go to a movie, and then go home and have a dinner of roast chicken with stuffing and gravy and cranberry sauce and cherry pie a la mode for dessert. Then the family would play with watercolors and puzzles and maybe read a book while classical music played in the background. I made fun of my fantasy and told my friend it was just a silly cliche of American life—an Ozzie and Harriet family fantasy.

The following Sunday was Father's Day. My friend, my daughter and I went to the playground, bought the Sunday paper, had an ice cream cone and then went to my friend's house where a surprise dinner awaited us. You can probably guess what she had cooked—the exact meal I had described to her the week before. I had made a wish. It had come true. It was a gift from a woman who loved me. Fantasy had become reality!

My reaction was to panic! I feared the woman was trying to get me to marry her. I thought she was trying to be a new mother for my daughter. I felt she was trying to take my freedom away — coming on too strong too fast. I was polite, distant, and quiet the entire evening.

A few weeks later we broke up. I cited some deficiency on her part as the reason, but deep down I knew the real reason: my inability to achieve intimacy with anyone had ruined yet another relationship. Her final words to me were that she had spent a year in ACoA and she recommended that I go to some meetings.

As a recovering person, I felt a bit of a renegade going to ACoA and talking about the ravages that alcoholics inflicted on me.

I was afraid of getting angry. I avoided anger like the plague because when I was a child anger in my family always led to violence. I was afraid ACoA would teach me to blame my parents. I didn't realize that, whether I faced it or not, there was already a lot of anger in me. It had just been stuffed deeper and deeper until it burst out in a thousand forms of negativity and defeatism and isolation and fear. I realized that no one was in the position to force me to blame my parents.

I am now allowing myself to feel the feelings that have never been felt. I must listen to the child within me that everyone else ignored. And if one of the feelings that comes up is blame, then I want to feel all there is to feel about blame. Then perhaps I can feel the anger behind the blame. And then the pain behind the anger. And the sadness behind the pain. And the acceptance rumored to lie behind the sadness. And the hope behind the acceptance. So that someday I may have a chance at leading a contented life.

It has been three years since I joined ACoA. The harsh, parental voice in my head severely criticizing everything I do has been stilled. I don't talk to myself in the abusive way my parents talked to me. I don't brutally punish myself for my mistakes the way my parents used to punish me. This has allowed me to take risks and to be creative in my recovery because I am on my side now. I have learned to parent myself the way I was never parented. And I am able to parent my daughter the way she deserves to be parented. I have become willing to go to any lengths to recover from the deprivation of my childhood.

The problems of my childhood created a huge stumbling block in the road to my recovery. I am truly grateful that ACoA was there when I was ready to address my childhood issues. I kept the shame and the pain of my childhood locked away for thirty-four years. With the help of ACoA I am unburdening myself of the trappings of the past, thereby creating room within me for new, exciting attitudes and feelings to enter. I look around the ACoA meetings and see a lot of my friends and I know I am not alone. I am grateful to be a part of the force of recovery which allows the chain of alcoholism which passes from generation to generation to be broken.

SEX AND VIOLENCE

There was a calmness in the house after the beatings. My father's orgasm of violence had occurred and he was temporarily spent. The air raids were over. There had been some damage, but no one had been killed. It was safe in the house until his horniness for violence mounted again. It was time to relax a bit and unclench our fists. Daddy was suddenly likeable and even playful. I think he saw what he had done. He saw us cowering from him. But he couldn't afford to have us stray from him, so he spent the following few days gathering his flock, wooing us back into the barnyard, combing our fleece, tidying up the nightmare, fluffing up our denial, fatting his little calves in preparation for the next slaying, for the next round of sacrifices, for the next shearing-off of our self-esteem.

We were trained to blame ourselves for the violence inflicted on us. We were trained to believe that we drove him to it. I blamed myself for the violence and I also blamed myself for returning to it time and time again. What else could I do? I was eight years old. I had to stay in the home, but I hated myself for lacking the courage to leave. I hated myself for not being able to stop the violence. I hated myself for not protecting my family from him by killing him. As an adult I hated myself for being so much like him. I hated myself for not killing myself because I was a likeness of him.

I was too afraid to kill myself so I did the next best thing. I placed myself in an alcoholic situation in which I could suffer all the indignities of death without killing myself. I did this by getting involved with women who didn't know how to love, by working for a man with a drinking problem, by recreating the family drama, which I hated but in which at least I knew the rules.

Today I am involved with the difficult task of changing my attitudes and behavior so that I can stop blaming myself for what happened. I am trying to stop hating and judging myself and my progress. I am trying to forgive myself for living, for that is not what I believed my father intended for me; therefore my very existence is a betrayal of my father's wishes. I am trying to keep myself out of alcoholic barnyards where I am treated like property. I am trying to celebrate having survived alcoholism. I am trying to celebrate having survived good times too, because they feel so new and I still don't feel that I deserve them.

But I do deserve the good times. I do deserve a good life. The war is over. I am cleaning up the mess. I am going to build my home on the site of the destruction. I am going to build a home in my heart for the little boy within me who survived the alcoholocaust.

I'M MEAN AND I'M TOUGH

I felt that I always had to be strong for my wife.
Whenever she saw any sign of weakness in me,
she would panic and the world would dissolve into
chaos. So I huffed and puffed and goose-stepped
my way through life. When I felt weak or tired
or vulnerable, I would hide it from her. I would
act mean and scare her away. I would sulk.
I would pretend to be busy writing. I would lie
to her about how I felt. And I became ill.

When I realized I couldn't live like that anymore,
and I began to show my vulnerability, she left.

I have heard that there really are people in the
world who won't reject you for being needy.
I find that hard to believe. But I have hope
that it is true. It would be nice to discover
such a person. But in the meantime I have
discovered that I will not reject me for being
needy. I do not call myself names or accuse
myself of self-sympathy if I find myself
crying or hiding or playing John Wayne.
I guess I have discovered a friend in me.
I find it hard to believe, but now that I am
better able to accept myself—I am not in
such a rush to find someone to do the
job for me.

DREAM NO. 109

My former wife, my daughter, and I were walking down a sidewalk at the edge of a large, very green yard. A man was being pulled across the yard by a large German Shepherd. The dog was mean and much stronger than the man.

The dog came at me with its mouth wide open. It was growling and ready to kill. I got my former wife and daughter safely out of the way. As the dog was about to bite me, I threw a copy of this book, *A Life Worth Waiting For!*, into its mouth. The dog bit the book instead of me.

The dog's master was very angry. He took the book out of the dog's mouth and flung it across the yard. I went and picked the book up. The back cover had been torn off. I put the book under my arm and walked away.

I approached a house at the edge of the yard. The house had a little outdoor shrine. It was blue and white and peaceful. There was a large, burning candle in front of some icon. I think it was the Virgin Mary. I took the candle and walked away with it, saying to the icon that I would return with it later. I woke up.

I sleepily stumbled into the kitchen and made myself a cup of coffee. I realized that this book has saved my life. It has saved me from the jaws of death and it has saved me from the jaws of my father. My father, who is German, was the Shepherd in my dream. The back cover was torn off because this book is not finished yet, although I thought it was. I took the candle from the icon as a symbol of my triumph, my salvation, my hope. I pledged to return the candle so that it would be there for the next person who needs it.

Everyone was safe, even the damn dog, who, despite the large teeth and immense strength, was unable to hurt me or the loved ones I protected, but whom I did not have to suffer for.

DREAM MOTORCYCLE

My father and I were driving down a perfectly straight desert highway. There were no trees, bushes, or buildings. There was nothing but the white hot road that we were traveling on at an incredible speed. My father was driving, steering with one hand and trying to push me out of the car with the other. I was terrified and fought with all my might to stay in the car, but I failed. I fell out, rolled like a tumbleweed, and got up, miraculously unhurt.

I wandered a while until I discovered a large, white, quaint country house. I began to introduce myself to a man who was working in his front yard, but I realized he already knew me, because in "real life" he was an employee of mine. He knew my plight without my having to say anything. We saw my father coming, and my friend directed me to some bushes on the side of the house where I could hide. My father walked into the house without knocking. He looked straight ahead and apparently didn't see me.

My friend kick-started a motorcycle that was sitting in the front yard. Without him saying anything to me, I knew that it was for me to escape on. I stood up and just as I was about to take the first step of running toward the motorcycle, my father lunged at me. He knew I was there all along. I avoided his grasp and ran toward the motorcycle, but before I could reach it I woke up—terrified!

. . • . .

I note with interest that my father was obviously acting with disregard for my life by trying to push me out of the car, but he was also being utterly reckless with his own life by not paying attention to his driving. We were racing at high speed toward oblivion on a long, straight, bleak road. My father was going down fast and he was trying to take me with him. His disease does not like to travel alone. I was pushed out of the car but managed to get away from my alcoholic father without too much damage. Feeling like a tumbleweed is not as desirable as feeling like, let's say, a swan, but a swan could not have survived in the desert of alcoholism, whereas a tumbleweed could roll with the cruel winds of abuse.

The white house represents my quest for a safe place. The man in the front yard shows me that I need help in escaping the ravages of alcoholism—that I cannot do it alone. It is interesting that I find a person I already know who can read my mind. This shows me how scared I am to ask for help, especially from someone new in my life.

I began the dream in a car, but ended it on a motorcycle. I am beginning to assume responsibility for the journey. I am on my own. I am driving, instead of my father. There is no room for him.

I sense freedom from my father, but the dream ends just as the journey is beginning. Traveling in the desert alone on a motorcycle is not easy. And even the illusory house with a white picket fence does not guarantee safety. I have made a break from my past. Illusions are being replaced with reality. I am on my way. There is no one there to push me off the motorcycle except—and hopefully not—me.

A BOTTOM OF SORTS

I am exhausted!
I have tried alcohol,
drugs,
sex, rock & roll,
poetry, travel, danger,
work, marriage,
money, parenthood,
spiritual literature,
self-help groups,
chiropractic,
therapy, sugar,
anger, coffee and
whole wheat muffins
to make me feel
real.

None of the best
or worst of these things
cured me of my
spiritual malady.
Now I am going to try
me. My Higher Power
and me.

THE FUN HAS BEEN CANCELED DUE TO A LACK OF INTEREST

I was supposed to attend a fun event tonight, but it was canceled due to a lack of interest. Things like this happen, and I think normal people might not be bothered that much by it, but it certainly caused a lot of pain in me.

As a child I became so used to aborted plans, vacation trips that never materialized, and promises that were always broken that I eventually shut down to any hope of good things to come. I was disappointed so many times I refused to get excited about anything. That was my way of avoiding disappointment.

So the cost of avoiding disappointment was to avoid joy. For little did I know that in order to suppress one feeling (disappointment), I had to suppress all feelings (like joy, anticipation, excitement).

In my life today, in order to be open to joy and excitement, I realize I have to be open to pain and disappointment. I cannot selectively edit which situations and feelings I will be an open, honest, and vulnerable man for. It is a package deal. I am open to life or I am not. I am sorry that things didn't work out for you tonight, Dwight. But I am proud of you for being willing to experience your life and the vast array of feelings that are becoming available to you as a result of your commitment.

DENY ME NOTHING

First I didn't want kids.
Then I didn't want pets.
Next I didn't want plants.
Eventually I rid myself of all
responsibility and all feelings
of belonging to anything including
myself. The absence of everything
meaningful in my life I called
freedom. I still didn't feel safe.
So I had a kid, bought a pet,
filled my house with plants.
I began to feel that I belonged
to everything I touched and
to everything that touched me.
Most of all I began to feel
I belonged to myself, and
to a world, not of my own
making, but of my own discovery.
I began to watch my life unfold
rather than trying to make it happen.
I feel safe because I belong here.
I rid myself of all feelings
of responsibility as a burden.
I embrace my responsibilities
because I am able to respond to life.
I want all life has to offer.
Deny me nothing.

FRAGMENTS

I am sitting here writing
thinking I should be playing guitar,
but if I were playing guitar
I would feel I should be writing.
Such is my need to feel wrong
and uncomfortable and inappropriate.

My life is like a car windshield
that has been struck by someone's head.
There is a point of impact
and a thousand shattered pieces
emanate from it.
Each piece of me
is in opposition to the others.
I am my biggest problem.

When you have had a headache all your life
and it is suddenly removed,
the absence of pain is intolerable.
Peace is boring.
Silence is deafening.
Serenity feels like death.

My persecutors have retired
from the business,
so I have assumed their position.
Until I can find a new line of work,
I search for new and different ways
to undermine my progress.

Like a food I've never tasted,
like a place I've never been,
good feelings are scary.
The power of recovery is awesome.
It will take some getting used to.
It will take some time.

I DIDN'T MEAN IT

If I am mean to me I will be mean to you. You, after all, appear to be an extension of me. To subject myself to merciless scrutiny means it will be your turn eventually. And then eventually you will turn away from me. You will have to. No one can take it forever.

To accept myself as I am means I will eventually become capable of accepting you for who you are. What a cozy circle. I treat myself with respect and dignity which allows me to treat you with respect and dignity which allows me to accept you treating me with respect and dignity because I have become familiar with being treated the way I deserve to be treated.

ICE AIN'T NICE

I stood outside the meeting room talking to a friend. "Are there any women in there?" I asked my friend. "Yeah, but they're too sick to play with you, baby," he replied.

He was right. I have been in recovery for six and one-half years now, and I have a strong feeling that I'm losing my sex appeal. Five years ago women approached me all the time in meetings. Now almost no one does. I thought I was doing something wrong. I thought recovery was turning me into a wimp as I became more in touch with my feelings, and therefore emotionally more vulnerable.

Another possibility is that when I was a beginner in recovery there were women who recognized me as an emotionally shut down man with whom they could play out their fear of abandonment. Their disease fell in love with my disease.

I am no longer shut down. My ability and willingness to show up for someone emotionally is very frightening to some people. So it seems that my feeling of being less attractive to these women is a sign of recovery. I am less attractive to sick women. That means I might be more attractive to healthier women. But I feel I am in a strange situation. The unavailable women I used to go for don't interest me anymore. Yet those women are the only ones I have ever gone out with. I wouldn't know a healthy women if I was involved with one. So the old way doesn't work anymore, yet there is not a new way intact to replace it.

I guess I just have to let it happen. These things have a way of taking care of themselves. Slowly I am getting healthier and, as I do so, healthier people are attracted to me. This is new terrain to me. Frightening. I'm afraid I will fall in love with a maelstrom again. End up walking arm in arm down the street with my disease thinking I'm fine and everything is peachy now that I have found love. I pray for faith that things can be different next time. I believe I have the insight to recognize when they're not. I feel I have the strength to get away from a bad situation if I find myself in one. I'm changing for the better.

SOMETIMES DOING NOTHING IS AN ACT OF COURAGE

A dead dog was lying in the road. The van that hit it was pulled to the curb. The driver was being ticketed by a police officer while another officer laid a yellow tarp under the dog and lifted it into the van. The dog's master was swaying back and forth, sobbing uncontrollably.

I became angry. "Why don't you sit in the van and cover your face if you are going to act like that! The dog is dead. It's over. Stop crying." Those were the words I heard myself saying silently in my head. The dog's master was experiencing grief and I couldn't handle it. His loved one had died tragically and his grieving was open and spontaneous. He didn't care who was watching or what they were thinking. His response was healthy and appropriate. I admired him for getting his feelings out, yet I was angry.

As I probed my heart to discover the nature of my conflicting emotions, I remembered how different my response to a similar situation had been twenty years earlier when I was a child. My father shot and killed my dog in a drunken moment of rage. I remembered feeling as if I'd been kicked in the stomach and the wind had been knocked out of me. And then I felt nothing. There were no tears. No words. No pain. Or so I thought. I thought that by refusing to succumb to the feelings of anger, loss, and remorse I was dealing with the problem. I thought I was taking it like a man.

In recovery I am learning to deal with my feelings in a more appropriate manner. It has not been easy or painless. I was raised with unhealthy ideas about what is appropriate. In my family it was appropriate to drink and to get violent, but it was definitely not appropriate at any time to cry. In recovery I am learning to accept feelings I cannot change. I am learning I will not be overwhelmed if I allow myself to feel sadness and loss. I am learning that if I want to experience a complete life, then I must be willing to accept sadness as well as joy. I am learning to sit and cry and try not to judge myself or my feelings until the sadness is lifted from me by my Higher Power. Sometimes doing nothing is an act of courage.

I have experienced the grief of separating from my wife and child. I felt grief over the loss of a friend who died. I felt grief over the loss of my old self—the self that could feel no pain and no joy, the self that was afraid to live and afraid to die, the self that could experience the loss of a pet and feel nothing, the self that I barely recognize any longer, the self that had to die so that I could be granted a new life.

I am learning to grieve without trying to masquerade my grief as anger or numbness, or trying to change it into bitterness in an attempt to make it hurt less. I am learning that grief is not negative in and of itself. It is my attitude toward it that is sometimes negative. It is yet another paradox that what I perceive as a loss is actually an opportunity to gain strength, compassion, understanding, and acceptance of the things that, if I allow myself to experience them, will bring me closer to being a contented human being.

UP UNTIL NOW

I was a
hand-wringing
lip-nibbling
knuckle-cracking
back-biting
guttersniping
eye-twitching
teeth-grinding
thumb-twiddling
little worry wart.
But now I am
perfect.
I think I'll
run for
Mayor
of New York City.

THE OBSCENE PHONE CALL

The phone rang. A woman introduced herself by saying that she had heard me speak and afterward had asked me for my phone number. She said she needed someone to talk to and even though I didn't remember her I was willing to listen. She talked about being lonely because she had just separated from her husband. She didn't know whether it was too soon to date or not. She missed having sex but was afraid of becoming intimate with someone because she didn't want to be hurt again. I enjoyed talking to her and actually saw the phone call as a godsend because she was dealing with a lot of the same issues I was. She enjoyed talking to me, she said, because I was easy to talk to, unlike a lot of the men she knew. That made me feel special and good.

I heard a lot of rustling sounds and asked her about them. She asked me to excuse her because she was changing into something more comfortable. She told me once again I was easy to talk to. Her honesty and openness was impressive. She began to get very blunt and specific about lovemaking. I felt a little queasy about some of the stuff she was saying but I saw it as somewhat of a breakthrough that I could talk that openly with a woman.

She became increasingly vulgar and obscene. I continued to listen. I really didn't know what I was feeling at that point. She asked me a totally disgusting question and I finally hung up the phone.

I clenched my right hand into a fist and placed the index finger knuckle into my mouth and bit down. I did this to avoid screaming because I was so angry. My daughter was asleep in the other room and I didn't want to wake her or I would have screamed. How dare that goon talk recovery to me in order to get me to open up so that she could exploit me all the while I was talking. I felt violated and abused—like I was being killed. Maybe I should never go to a meeting or speak again. Maybe I ought to change my telephone number—or change my name. I felt like I was being punished for confiding in another human being, that this was evidence that "silence is golden" and communicating is filthy. I thought of that woman, cozy and satisfied and comfy, while I was pulling my hair out because of her and all I did to deserve it was to answer the phone and try to help someone in pain. I thought about my mother. I hated my mother at that moment. I hated her almost as much as I hated myself. I was very confused. First I had to deal with a sicko on the phone and then suddenly the sicko didn't seem as significant as my mother and me. Why?

I never knew if I was supposed to be my mother's son or her psychiatrist or her neighbor or her boyfriend or her husband or her father or her banker or her butler or her pastor. I guess I was supposed to be all these things and more to her. Most of all, I was supposed to listen. And I had to listen to the most outrageous stuff you've ever heard. I had to listen to stories about how Millie down the block stuffed her bra. I had to hear about how my father came back from India with venereal disease. I had to listen to how the neighbor gave my mother a ride home from the bar because my father refused to leave and on the way home the neighbor put his hand on my mother's leg now what did I think of that? Then she would sit there blank-faced waiting for an answer. I was eight years old and she was sitting there waiting for an answer. I would fumble for something to say. "That wasn't very nice," I said, hoping those words would comfort my poor mother. I had to listen to how everyone who wasn't a whore was a bastard. Then I had to listen to how important it was to keep the faith in Jesus.

And so I grew up and forgot about these things, and eventually I become a parent—and a good one at that—and it is Sunday night

and I am about to go to bed and the phone rings and there is a
sicko on the line telling me all that crap and I hate myself for listening. I feel utterly unable to move. Because that obscene
woman on the phone is like my mother and my job is to listen and
listen and listen. I felt I had no choice but to sit there and listen to
that drunken, insane, garbage talk. I thought that by listening to
that stuff I was being a good son. And so along comes another
abusive alcoholic with a disgusting, abusive rap and, just like a little boy, I listen to her. I would kill and maim people to protect my
daughter from listening to that, but I expose myself to it. I was
angry with myself that I was not a good parent to myself.
I couldn't get off the phone because she was in pain and, being
a good little boy, I couldn't walk away until she was satiated and
she wasn't satiated until she abused me for her own needs. I was
angry at myself because I took it. I voluntarily took another heap-
ing of abuse. This taking of abuse is deeply woven into every
fiber of my spirit. It is in every chromosome of my body. It is so
much a part of me I couldn't see it. Until now.

. . • . .

A few months passed. The phone rang. It was the same women.
"You might not remember me," she said, as I listened to the sound
of bath water sloshing around in the background, "but I heard you
speak once and you gave me...."

"I remember you," I said. "You might not remember having called
me before but you did, and the last time we talked I felt violated.
We started talking about recovery and you ended up masturbat-
ing. I felt used and abused. You abused me enough that I cannot
ever have a conversation with you again. I don't trust you. You
hurt me enough that I was almost unable to talk to or trust anyone
else. I can't talk to you." There was a long pause. "I don't know
what to say," she finally said, "except that I respect you." She
hung up.

I stood still with the receiver in my hand for a long time. I felt
great. I saw the second phone call as a gift from my Higher

Power. Only a few months had lapsed between the calls from her, and yet by the time of the second call I had worked through enough of the feelings about the first call that I was no longer in a place where I felt I had to listen to the abuse. And I didn't have to attack that sick woman in order to stand up for myself. I paid attention to myself and my needs and dismissed her and her needs. I'm growing up. I realize I am no longer the prisoner of my past. I am more selective of what I expose myself to. I don't stand still and let people dump their stuff on me anymore. If a conversation turns abusive, I will turn and walk away in the middle of a sentence if I want to. I am more careful about whom I share myself with. I can see abuse coming a mile away now. I can hear it in a tone of voice. I can stop it before it like a cancer grows. I sense freedom.

I hung up the phone and went to bed.

GHOSTS

ghosts
in my head
wish I were dead.

there is the ghost
of how it used to be
reminding me of the misery
and convincing me of the
futility
of trying to get to the
center of me.

there is the ghost
of a child within
who wants to live again
a child who for thirty years
has nightly whispered in my ear:
come play with me
I never get to play
am I supposed to be alone
is that why you went away?

there is a ghost
in this room right now
that is telling me to
roll over and play dead
this ghost always talks to me
like I'm a dog
this ghost has the voice of my
father
howling and growling and
telling me I'm selfish
whenever I try to

communicate with anyone.
these ghosts
that live rent-free in my head
and wish I were dead
are secretly looking
for another place to live:
be on guard, my friend,
they are lousy tenants,
noisy, never clean up after
themselves, and are desperate
because they see me
walking toward them
with eviction papers
in my hand.

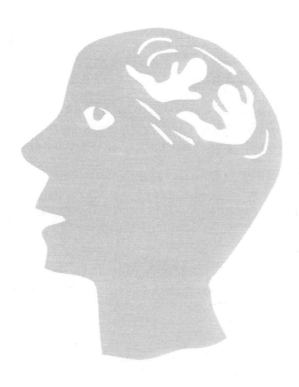

HERE'S TO YOUR HEALTH

I hate being a beginner. Whenever I start anything new I feel like a child, full of potential but with little actualization of my dreams and ambitions. Being a beginner feels like a weakness; like an admission of imperfection, of vulnerability, of dependence on the guidance of others.

As a child I was taught not to show any signs of weakness, lest I be taken advantage of. "It is at the point of the weakest link that you might be attacked," I was told, so I learned to conceal what I didn't know. I managed to protect myself rather well. But I rarely learned anything new.

Being a beginner is fearful stuff. Some people thrive on competition. Others don't. I am an "other." Faced with stiff competition, I get scared. I squander my energy. My friends who enjoy competing with other men tell me that their adrenaline, concentration, and energy all come together when set to a challenge. I lapse into confusion. I manage to compete. But my success is tempered by bouts of self-doubt, fear of failure, and fear of the judgment of my peers. And yet I have managed a certain level of success in two careers I engage in simultaneously. I have done it by avoiding competition and the negative feelings it conjures up.

I like to start at the top. I will practice at home forever, preparing myself for the day when I can walk into a new place and everyone will assume that I have been there for years. I am allergic to the word "rookie." I am addicted to the word "pro." When I avoid the clumsy steps in between, and try to learn the ropes in secret, no one is fooled except me.

* * * * *

You can imagine the resistance I had to joining a health club at the age of thirty-six. I began with an aerobics class. Out of a class of twenty-seven people, I was the only man. I was also about ten years older than everyone else. I was the least adept person in the class, which is another way of saying I didn't know what I was doing. The other members would clap their hands together twice, touch the palm of each hand to the floor while keeping the legs only slightly bent, do some motions with their arms that looked like swimming out of water, and then they were off! Three steps forward! Clap! Two to the right ! Clap twice!! Jog backwards three steps with the knees brought up high! Duck and twirl 360 degrees! Walk to the left with the hips facing forward!

"Shake it out!" the instructor commanded. Shake what out? I thought to myself. I felt like a pedestrian dodging traffic at rush hour on Lexington Avenue in midtown. "Come on, girls, let's do it!!!" The instructor said in a euphoric frenzy, making me feel even worse.

I was able to laugh at myself and my inability to keep up. The laughing stopped, however, when I tried to leave after the class was over and I had to hold onto the rail on my way down the stairs. My arms were shaking so bad I had to quit trying to comb my hair because I kept sawing my ear and raking my nose. I went to a restaurant and held my glass of water with two hands. "Don't watch," I said to the waitress who was trying to figure out what my problem was.

I actually felt great, despite the pain, because I knew the ice had been broken. I was on my way! I had made a commitment to my health and to the willingness necessary to do what it takes, even if it meant torturing myself in a room full of women in order to become physically fit.

It wasn't long before I was doing aerobics three times a week. I began working on the fitness machines three times a week as well. It was becoming a part-time job to get into shape. After a few months I took another step and moved into the weight-lifting room. It was there that a lot of my old feelings about being a beginner and competing with other men came up again with an intensity I had not felt since childhood.

In the locker room I saw myself as a tall, thin, pale, thirty-six-year-old beginner surrounded by a sea of young, muscular, tan, human body machines. I stuck out like a carrot in a watermelon display. Here were all the bullies of my elementary school years, all grown up and meaner and tougher than ever. Their veins bulged out like highways on a roadmap. All the Paul Bunyans of the world were there. Looking at them gave me the strangest sensation that I was shrinking. I had the temptation to show them my gold card, or my resume, or a picture of my girlfriend, or anything to help me regain my dwindling ego. I puffed up my chest and held my breath as I walked around, but I could only do that for so long until I had to let the air out. I felt like a bagpipe at the end of a song. I draped myself in towels, one around my waist and one around my shoulders. I kept my eyes downcast. I looked like a wet guru.

There was nowhere to hide. As Bob Dylan once said, "Sometimes even the President of the United States must have to stand naked." I had gone to extremes to keep these men from finding out what they already knew. I was a beginner.

· · • · ·

A few weeks later I was parading around the locker room naked and as comfortable as if I were at home alone. I was still tall and thin and pale, but I also felt proud and handsome and hopeful. How did this happen?

For one thing, time. As time passes, you become comfortable with new situations. I saw my extreme self-consciousness whittled away by self-acceptance. I am who I am. Period. No one seemed to really care whether I was a beginner or not. I was the only one making a big deal out of it. So I dropped it.

I also began to directly address that little boy in me who was so frightened of competition and of the feelings associated with being a beginner. I allowed the child within me to begin at the beginning. I allowed him the right to be clumsy and awkward, to learn to walk before he learned to run. I gave him the right to ask stupid questions and I told him, "The only stupid question is one that isn't asked."

I allow myself my own definition of what a man is. And it doesn't have much to do with muscles or machismo. I realize now that I can feel masculine, aggressive, and competitive without feeling in danger of becoming an ogre. I can be large in stature without being dominating. I can be tough without being mean. I can be strong without being tyrannical. I can also be open and vulnerable without being a wimp. I can become a new man of my own making according to more flexible and creative standards. Working out in a health club got me in touch with my own maleness.

I have learned that I can compete against myself and no one else. It is what I think of myself that is important. Other people are welcome to their opinion of me and my performance. What they think of me is none of my business. It is much easier to make progress as a beginner if I can stay in my own head and out of other people's. This allows me to set my own goals and achieve them at my own pace. I have realistic expectations of myself based on my own performance, free of comparison with what the handsome hedonist next to me is doing.

As a result of focusing on myself, I am gradually beginning to believe in me and my abilities. The lessons are so clear and immediate in a health club. Exceed your limits and you get hurt. Have a positive attitude and a reverence for your body, and you can stretch your boundaries beyond anything you ever dreamed possible for yourself.

I listen closely to my instructor and freely ask for help and advice. All of the instructors are younger than me. At thirty-six I am beginning to see this phenomenon more often. Police officers, doctors, bosses—all younger than me. It is new and not easy for me to take orders and criticism from younger men. But it is a fact that my instructor knows a lot more than I do. It takes humility to get my ego out of the way and not take the criticism personally. I hate it when I reach for a weight and my instructor sees me from across the room and says aloud, "A wee bit too ambitious for today, don't you think, Dwight?" But I know he has my best interest at heart.

My body is a temple and my instructor and I are working at building it together. My health is a communal effort. People in the club help each other by sharing ideas and equipment. I have many teachers. I take the advice I want and discard the rest.

I am learning that I can be disciplined without being obsessive. I can be dedicated without being a slave. I have learned to be playful within the realm of serious work. I can miss a session without feeling like a failure. I have learned how to give myself some slack. I shoot for an eighty-five percent performance so as to avoid the unhappy trappings of perfectionism.

I allow myself to endure a little pain. I have always avoided pain at any cost. But growth is sometimes painful. Progress is often frustrating and nearly invisible. The tendency is often to push yourself too hard. The mind often wants to progress at a rate that the body isn't capable of. This tryanny is often justified by the slogan "No pain, no gain." I use a substitute slogan, "Listen to your body—it is trying to tell you something." I do not have a master/slave relationship with my body. I view my body as an ally and I treat it with respect. I am careful not to inflict unnecessary pain.

* * * * *

I joined a health club because I didn't want to be winded walking up a flight of stairs. I also wanted to do something about my weight. And I wanted to meet some healthy people. I didn't want to follow in the footsteps of a very dear friend who died suddenly and unexpectedly from a heart attack. Desire for health, fear of illness, and loneliness led me to the door of the club.

As my body began to change, I realized that the club membership began as a physical manifestation of a spiritual journey. My story is not only about working out. It is about living. Working out increases my hunger for food. It also increases my hunger for life. All the lessons I have learned in my health club are directly applicable to many other areas of my life.

I have found physical health. I feel much more comfortable living in my body than I ever have before. Other things are happening. My diet is better. My self-esteem is increasing. I'm more outgoing. I have a more open and honest way of communicating with other people. I have found the stereotypes about muscle men to be as misleading and false as stereotypes about any other group of people. I have found an environment in this difficult city where it feels safe to strike up conversations with women. I have found friends.

If you had known me a handful of years ago, you would never have guessed I would be working out in a health club today. I spent more time underground than a carrot. But I have been uprooted by a massive national movement toward health. I feel young. I feel better about myself than ever before.

I am becoming a man I admire and respect. Not only has this progress been rewarding, it has been fun. I insist on enjoying the difficult process of building my body to my own liking. Sometimes I resent the time it takes. Sometimes I regret that I didn't start ten years earlier. I get over these feelings. I started when I started because that was when I was ready to start. I enjoy it. It is time well spent. I always feel better about myself after each session. It takes courage to change. It takes courage to be a beginner. It takes courage to stand shoulder to shoulder with the big boys. I give myself credit for that.

CRIPPLE

In the middle of my aerobics class, I heard the voice of a child screaming inside me, "I am not a cripple!" I continued wiggling my butt and dancing around in rare aerobic form while I said to myself, "It's true! The child lives on within me!"

My Higher Power had offered me a precious revelation. I had been crippled for five years as a child. I didn't learn to walk and run until I was seven. And, like a dog with a wounded leg, I have favored my leg ever since. My leg had fully recovered from the disease when I was a little boy, but I had continued until I was thirty-five to treat myself like a cripple. Life was more a matter of what I was to avoid doing rather than what I was to do.

It was not just my legs that I treated this way. I treated myself as if I were mentally and spiritually handicapped. I believed I had a gimpy leg and a gimpy mind and a gimpy spirit. I was always trying to play it safe, as if taking a risk would kill me. But constantly settling for less than what I wanted and deserved was not safe at all. The real killer was rage over not getting what I thought I needed.

Now I try to think of myself as a man becoming whole. I am not a cripple. I am not sick. I am becoming. I am evolving. I am dissolving old lies my parents told me and I told myself. My aerobics is a dance of celebration. I celebrate the process of becoming. I want the little boy within me who thinks he is still crippled to come out and join me in the celebration. I once was lame, but now I walk. With solid feet on solid ground, I am walking toward the light within me.

A NOTE IN THE MAIL

My pajamas (canary yellow)
are freshly laundered
neatly folded
waiting in a drawer
for you to come over
and put them on once more.

ALMOST NUMB

Occasionally
my humanity
appears like a bubble
under the varnish
of an otherwise perfect
denial.

GETTING EVEN

I take what doesn't belong to me
in an attempt to even the score.
No matter what the good Lord gives me
I'm always searching for more.

THERE IS NOTHING I CAN DO

If it is meant to happen
there is nothing I can do to stop it.
If it is not meant to happen
there is nothing I can do to make it.

I AM ENOUGH

Tell all the people that you meet
my life is complete
when I'm alone.
I don't need a loved one coming around
wearing a frown
turning my life upside down.

I am enough to get me through.
I don't need you
to show me the way.
You've had your say.
Now go away.
I am enough.

Wait a minute!
What is this stuff
tumbling down my face?
What a disgrace!
Is it a sign of the pain
of running a race
against myself,
putting everyone on a shelf
and trying to make a home
by living alone?

Isolation is no part-time job.
I don't know if I am
tough enough for this.
I have to admit
I'm in a fit of loneliness.
I wish to brush it away
like cookie crumbs on my lap.
I want to take a nap, wake up,
and find the perfect lover beside me.

I can't hide me from the world anymore.
I want to be a part of it.

I want to have a human face
and be part of the human race
and realize it is no disgrace
to want to be loved.

I am enough!
I'm on my side.
I can walk with pride and dignity.
I have cast off the wet blankets
of pity and confusion I once wore.
My feet are firmly on the floor
and my heart reaches toward heaven.
My ear is pressed against the door
which leads to a new life.

Because I am enough
I am ready for love.
I can find you without losing me.
I have found my identity
as a strong and wonderful man
who can take you by the hand
without pulling you along.

I am ready for love!
I can respect you as a person
because I can respect me as a person.
You are my mirror which reflects life.
I treat you as I treat myself
and I am beginning to treat myself
quite well.
I can tell because I am ready for love.
Let me shout it out:
I am ready for love!

And lucky be
the woman who finds me.

MONDAY MORNING IN NEW YORK

Today the air smells
like snow tastes.

Lexington Avenue
is a meadow
where people waver
like windblown
golden wheat.

A tree in front
of a skyscraper
imagines itself
a forest.

Lonely shoes
in a store window
look longingly at me
like puppies
in an animal shelter
their tongues wagging
waiting for adoption.

Goldfish swim
in a curbside
puddle.

Hope crackles
like peanut shells
under my feet.

The prettiest woman
at the bus stop
just sat next to me
and is reading this
as I write it.

Are you busy
Saturday night?

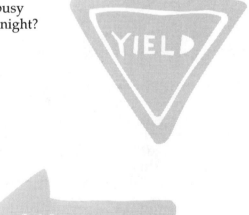

EEK! ANOTHER BIRTHDAY

I just had a birthday and I don't like it. I have not liked my age for the last six years in a row. I have a right to not like my age so don't try to talk me out of it.

I must admit, however, that I am in much better shape than, let's say, ten years ago. I am physically, emotionally, and spiritually younger. At twenty-six I was a defeated old man. At thirty-six I am well into a recovery that has not only repaired a lot of the damage, but has actually restored me to a condition that is better than the condition I was in in the first place. I have learned to turn back the hands of time.

I do not feel I have been granted a new life. Because I do not feel I had a life to begin with. I now feel like I have been born for the first time. I guess what I had before recovery was an existence. I existed. Now I have a life. I live. It is a blessing to know there is a difference between existing and living.

Recovery has served me an appetizer that is most delicious. It has stirred in me an appetite for life that is amazing. I have never known such a hunger. I understand the main course is about to be served. I am excited and curious and hopeful. Recovery has taught me the difference between devouring life and dining on it. I take small bites, chew well, and savor. When I become full I stop, knowing that there will be enough for Dwight when it is time to partake once more.

I am moving in at least two different directions at once. My body is getting older, but I take better care of it so I feel younger. I am becoming wiser as I learn and grow, but I am simultaneously nurturing the child within me so I feel wise yet childlike. I am becoming more mature as I learn to face and accept my emotions but I am not as bogged down with dogma, defeatism, and clinging to my pain, so the effect is to feel that I am maturing and becoming lighter at the same time. I no longer feel that I am rowing my psychic boat upstream all the time. I feel like I am floating on a gentle river of time. As I move away from my youth, I move closer to myself.

Today I am the exact age God wants me to be. My age is yet another thing I am powerless over. My job when it comes to my age is the same job when it comes to anything else—I must learn to accept myself as I am. I must learn to love myself for who and what I am. It has been a good year. The evolution continues. Happy birthday to Dwight.

GULPING LIFE

Some people gulp life,
chugging it
until more runs down
their chins
than gets inside them.
I am one of those people.
Don't even know
what I'm drinking
or why.

I want to learn to
sip at
and savor life,
breathe deeply while
I'm drawing it in.
I want to know
what it is I'm ingesting.

When you gulp and
chug life,
it is only when
the glass is empty
that you smack
your lips and say
"What was that?"

Ah, but when you
savor life
and dare to take it
in little sips,
accepting your thirst,
allowing yourself to be
filled slowly,
you become more than
filled.
You become
fulfilled.

Savoring life has
created a thirst in me
for more life.
I fear not an empty glass.
For it is only when the
glass is empty
that it can be
fulfilled again.

WHAT IS RIGHT FOR ME

Hope hovers
above the treetops
like a fog
which I stroll through.
Promise,
like a mat of moss,
comforts my every step.
Faith, like a dew,
covers everything.
Love,
like my refrigerator,
hums incessantly,
waiting to be opened.
Fate waits for me
to play my part.
Only I can
blow it.

Only I can
call purity pollution
call love domination
call faith servitude
call devotion slavery.

Bodies in motion
tend to stay in motion.
I am moving closer
to what is right for me.
It is true that
I am the problem
but I am also the solution.

IN MEMORY OF JOSEPH SCOTT

Into the Kingdom of Heaven this day has entered a good man. His name is Joseph Scott. He was my friend for six years. We entered a recovery program at the same time and thus were like childhood friends watching each other grow. Later he became my voice teacher and walked me into the world of music. I was lost within myself and afraid to be seen or heard for fear of being ridiculed or rejected. He took the little boy within me and gave him a voice. He instilled confidence in me to stand up and be heard. He was unfalteringly supportive of me. He never tried to talk me out of my feelings or moods. He accepted me and loved me as I am. He listened so intently it startled me. He fixed the gaze of his bright, clear eyes on me and listened with a singleness of mind and without judgment. Sometimes I would come for a lesson and there would be very little singing. We pretended the lessons were only about singing, but they were really about life.

I will never forget the many times I walked into his large apartment in the Ansonia Hotel. The door was never locked. I rang the bell and walked in. Birds flew free around the living room. He had a piano in his studio. The top of which was littered with recital invitations, greeting cards, photographs, and a copy of one of my poems. I was so proud he chose to keep my poem on top of his piano for all his students to see. He was a member of the American Orchid Society and his apartment was full of them. One orchid plant was huge and had four stalks and was a gift from me. He was a collector of crystals and quartz and, instead of books, in the bookcases the shelves were scattered with shells and gems. He had crystals hanging in the windows and prisms would dance their rainbows of light along the walls of the studio while we sang. I always brought an apple for the teacher and placed the offering on his piano. I began the practice of bringing the apple almost as a joke. But it soon became a ritual. I saw the apple as a good omen, a symbol of the purity of our friendship. Twice I brought my four-year-old daughter to my lesson so that she too could bask in the friendship of this special man. I will greatly miss his studio, with its array of empty chairs, and its orchids and birds and crystals.

And I will miss him. We were friends. He was so good to me, and I am proud to say that I was good to him. Several times I treated him to dinner in a fancy restaurant, knowing that we shared a fondness for good food and we both heralded from that bastion of great American cooking, Louisiana. I spent last Christmas Day visiting him in the hospital where I was amazed at his positiveness and good spirits. I am grateful that I have no regrets about the way I treated him. I am grateful that I can say I was as good to him as he was to me.

I am sorry Joseph is dead. I am sorry for myself. Heaven is a better place today because Joseph Scott is there. But I am here on earth with the memory of him. I cry for me. And for all the people who knew him. I was truly blessed by having him in my life and now he is gone and I miss him terribly. I miss his grey beard and his voice as big as New York. I miss him because I know how few men there are of his stature. Knowing him makes me appreciate the value of friendship, and the scarcity of true friendship.

Friendships have never been easy for me. Joseph knew that.
I was always holding back my love from everyone, including him. I would try to conceal my pain, but I could never fool Joseph. He could sense my pain and would draw it out of me, urging me to share it with him. Often I would not. One day he hugged me. I felt myself get very tense and rigid. I tried to pull away. And the damnest thing happened. He wouldn't let me. He hugged me and hugged me and hugged me until all the resistance and anger and distance dissolved into trust. When he had hugged me to the point of love and trust and vulnerability, he let me go. He smiled at me, told me to be good to myself, and then threw me out because his next student was waiting. He had a way of pulling the goodness out of me, of bringing my love to the surface.

Yesterday I was on the bus, riding to work. I was silently weeping, having heard just the night before about Joseph's death.

A woman named Jennifer whom I barely know, and who does not know Joseph, sat beside me. I did not want her there. I was devastated by my feelings for Joseph and I wanted to be alone. She said to me, "Look at this." She opened her hand and in the palm of it lay a large crystal. Without thinking I opened my mouth and these words came out, "You don't know what this is doing to me! I just finished writing in my journal that Joseph was a man made of crystal and you show me this! Joseph's house was full of crystal and he firmly believed in their healing power. Is this a message from Joseph that everything will be alright? Were you sent by Joseph?" She, of course, didn't know exactly what I was talking about, but she did say, "Do you really think a man such as you just described to me can die?" I replied first with silence. Then I said, "No. A loving spirit cannot be created or destroyed; it can only be transformed. I cannot fathom that a life force such as that embodied in Joseph Scott is destroyed simply because the earthly body withers. I have sensed him with me ever since I received the news of his death and I sense him with me now."

I do not know and I do not care if other people think my belief is uncanny or impossible. But I know Joseph is with us now. I know I will carry a little bit of his love and his lesson with me forever. I was blessed with his presence in my life. Long live Joseph Scott. My brother. My friend. My teacher. My mentor. My power of example.

A LARGE LESSON WRAPPED IN A SMALL PACKAGE

The tears streamed down my face as I sat in the memorial service for my friend Joseph Scott. I was scared and embarrassed. I had only cried a few times in my life, and never in public. I felt powerless over my tears, unable to control them. I didn't know how they started and I didn't know how and if they would ever end. I closed my eyes and let the crying happen.

I had never felt such immense grief. I opened my eyes and saw a woman begin to sob and lean her head upon the shoulder of the man she was with. I felt so lonely. My dear friend was dead. I wanted someone to comfort me. I wanted someone to hold my hand. I fantasized a woman I love very much, but who is no longer with me, holding my hand. The fantasy helped for only a brief moment because to myself I said, Who are you kidding, Dwight? She is not here. She doesn't want you.

A voice in my head said, But God is here. God wants you. Why don't you ask God to hold your hand? So I did.

I reached down to the pew where a book of hymns lay. I wrapped my hand around the book. And felt comforted. God was my comfort in my hour of grief.

I thought the death of my friend was such a terrible thing. But I am learning so much from it. I guess it took the death of my friend and the extremely painful aloneness I felt while I sat in the pew listening to him being eulogized by the people who loved him—I guess it took that for me to realize that I can turn to myself and to God for what I need. There was nowhere else for me to turn. There was no woman, no meal, no money, no drug, no fantasy that could save me from myself. The death of Joseph has drawn me into friendship with myself and God. All the reaching outward to fill my spiritual needs has been exposed for what it is—reaching away from the source of spiritual fulfillment.

Nothing earth-shattering has happened as a result of my revelation of God as my comforter. But something has changed. I don't know exactly what it is and I don't need to know. I am satisfied with feeling that I have moved closer to God and therefore I have moved closer to myself, which is the key to moving closer to you. And that is what I want to do. The feeling is that I truly love you but that love is locked within a prison of fear. My fear is the lock. But God is the key. I am coming out of myself and moving into the world. I smell freedom. I want to live.

FOUR PRAYERS

Dear God
help me to realize and accept
that no human being can fill
this neediness in me.
My need is so great
I could devour the love and strength
of a continent of people
and still feel unloved and lonely.
Dear God fill this need in me
with your boundless love.
Help me to realize
my need will be filled
from many sources, by many friends.
I don't have to
seek everything
from one person
who is bound to fail me
because that person
is not you.

Dear God
Help me to see
that this longing
I feel
is a longing
for you
which is a longing
for me.

Help me to see
that this wanting
I feel
is a wanting
to be
with you
which is a wanting
to be
with me.

God deliver me
from this misery.
I'm too blind to see
the self-pity
that imprisons me.
Please deliver me
from this emergency
and let me be
a child unto Thee.

Dear God, please forgive my lack of trust in you. I believe in you. But I don't trust you. I want to trust you. But I don't. I suffer because I don't trust you, but knowing that doesn't stop the lack of trust.

I remember as a child I would walk out onto the balcony and look up at the stars and my heart would overflow with love for you while the screaming and sound of my father's fist connecting with my mother's face provided background music to my prayers. I did not understand why you let it happen, and I knew there must be a reason, so I did not let it shake my faith in you. After all, you had granted me recovery from being physically crippled for five years. But there I was, emotionally crippled by an illness that mercilessly rampaged through my family and you didn't stop it. My faith began to wane.

I became an adult and was stricken with the same disease that had afflicted my parents. The insanity I had witnessed became the insanity I possessed. It felt like the cruelest of fates. I stood in the middle of a rainy French Quarter street, shaking my fist heavenward and howling my hatred of you like a wounded dog. I turned my back on you. I turned my back on me. I raced like a child on a slide into the pool of my addiction. Life without you has been very cold. And lonely.

I thought you would punish me if I told you these things, as if you didn't already know them. But the God of my understanding as I know Him today is a friend of mine. I want to share ALL my feelings with you. You are the God I believe in and love. You are also the God I fear and do not trust. And you are the God without whom I cannot salvage my life from the wreckage of the past. Please guide me in my struggle for a new life. And please understand me as my old self clings to its spiritual sickness. Please forgive my resistance as you gently pry my fingers from the illusion I desperately cling to.

I have been away from you for such a terribly long time. I want to come home. Thanks for waiting so patiently and keeping the light on. I feel warm and hopeful. Amen.

TASTE THE FIRE

I was crippled for five years as a child.
Result: I became a poet. And I have new joy
in the discovery, at the age of thirty-six,
of my body and all its wondrous abilities.

I was an alcohol- drug- and gift-abuser
in my twenties.
Result: I have a new life—it's not like being
reborn, but like being born for the first
time, with a fresh vision, childlike and
sweet, eager and curious.

My marriage failed. I found myself a single
parent, alone and scared with a two-year-old
daughter looking to me for direction
at a time when I was lost.
Result: I am a better parent than I ever
would have been had I remained hiding in a
numb marriage, having moored myself to a
woman so I would not have to venture out
into the stormy sea of self-discovery.
As I raise my daughter, so I raise myself.
It is a sad and beautiful and scary and
fun and magnificent journey. I have a bond
with my daughter that even death is
powerless to break.

I was raised by two sick people who taught
me insanity and fear and hatred. I was
raised in hell. Chaos felt like home.

Result: I learned to land on my feet in
any situation. I can stand face to face
with the cruelest of ogres. The walls of
my world cracked apart and through them
I saw another reality. I became a seeker.
I learned the taste of fire. I felt the
pain of birth. I carry the torch of freedom
for my ancestors, victims all of the plague
which has spared me. I have met myself.
I have met my Maker. I break bread with the
child within me. I have tasted my own tears.
I have learned to look beyond the pain.
I have learned to respect this unusual life.

Without my parents this book would not have
been written.

MY FATHER MEETS MY DAUGHTER

I always felt as if I had no ancestors. I never met any of my relatives. I'm still not sure what a cousin is. I never met my grandparents. I always wondered what they were like. I felt disconnected. I didn't want that to happen to my daughter. My parents are old and ill now. Time is running out. I wanted them to see my beautiful daughter. I wanted them to see what a good job I am doing as a single parent. I wanted them to know that the two generations they left in their wake are doing just fine. So I took my five-and-a-half-year-old daughter to meet her grandparents.

We walked from the plane to the airport terminal and looked around expectantly. There was no one there to greet us. I called my parents' home. My father was shaving, getting ready to come and pick us up. Once again, in a literal sense, my father was not there for me. I didn't make a big deal out of it, but I allowed myself to feel the disappointment I had tried to deny for most of my life. All the other passengers had claimed their baggage and left. We stood waiting in a sweltering parking lot for him to arrive.

My father showed up a little while later looking thin and flabby. Time has not been nice to Daddy. Nor has Mr. Booze. The brawn of his youth has turned to gelatin. His spirit has dwindled like beer foam. He was not the Paul Bunyan of a man I somehow always pictured him to be. I wonder if he ever was? I could detect no emotion whatsoever coming from him as he greeted me and my daughter. It was a somewhat formal greeting.

On the way to his house I asked him if we could stop at a store so I could buy my mother some flowers. My father offered to pay for them. I thought that was a strange request. He never reached for his wallet, leading me to believe that he never intended to pay for them. But he seemed to have some need to take away the power of my gift, to subvert my generosity, as if buying flowers for my mother did not fit into his conception of me.

We entered the house and my first impression was of dirt and darkness. The air smelled as if the windows had not been opened for fifty years. We were directed into our room, which was in total disarray. The room was filthy. I told myself that my parents were sick people who had a hard time getting around and that was why the place was such a mess. But I gave them two months notice that we were coming. They had two months to open a window and vacuum the floor of the unused bedroom before their granddaughter came to visit for the first time. I guess it takes more than two months or two years or even two generations to vacuum all traces of insanity and neglect out of a home. They say the state of your house reflects the state of your mind. A clean, fresh house would have been totally out of character for them.

There had been no preparation for our arrival. I am not saying that my father should have hired a brass band to herald our homecoming, but it seems that my parents thought about our arrival only when the phone rang and we were at the airport. I began to feel foolish and wrong. There I was in New York getting a haircut and braiding my daughter's hair and there were my parents not even thinking about our arrival. I could see that my old habit of turning uncomfortable situations against myself was activated again. I noticed one bed was made and one was not. I wondered who the unmade bed was for. Who wasn't welcome?

My daughter and I went to the pool and she began to swim. She was having a wonderful time. I went into the apartment and asked my father to come to the pool so I could take a picture of him with his granddaughter. They sat on a bench. My father sat as far away from her as he could. There was no sign of any feeling. There was no attempt to tickle her or pat her on the head. I took the picture. Through the lens he looked like a cactus growing in the desert: parched, arid, prickly, unmovable. Before I pushed the button I said to myself, If he sees this picture he is going to hate it. I wish I could convince the camera to lie a little—teach it denial. I wish I could teach the camera how to make my father look younger, make him look friendly and excited and full of love of life and children. I wish the camera could make him look proud of me.

A little while later Celeste and I went back into the apartment. Celeste went into the kitchen to talk to her grandfather and I went into my mother's room. My mother was so pale and so sick and so bent over and so whacked out on Valium that it was quite impossible to talk to her. She kept getting lost in the sitcom on television. I think she kept confusing me with one of the characters on the screen. I said to her, "Mom, I came here because I wanted you to know that I am doing well and Celeste is doing well and I am a good father and there is nothing for you to worry about." She wasn't the slightest bit worried. The Valium took care of that. I thought she would be excited to see me for the first time in five years. She had never known me since I became a father. I thought she would be excited about her granddaughter. No luck.

In the background I could hear my daughter talking with my father. He was telling her that he could hear the chickens in the pot screaming, "Let me out! Let me out!" Now you know where I got my weird sense of humor. My father was actually enjoying the company of my daughter. I was amazed. And pleased. I thought there might be some validity to my suspicion that there is some remote trace of emotional life left in my father. My mother seems to be emotionally dead. I don't think a feeling has surfaced in her in thirty years. My father seems to be merely emotionally buried alive.

It was getting late, past my daughter's bedtime. Dinner was nowhere in sight, so I fed Celeste pieces of cheese and whatever I could get my hands on in the refrigerator. I put my daughter to bed just as my father was getting my mother out of bed. The process of preparing dinner was carried on forever, just like it was when I was a kid. No one really eats. We pick at food, like pigeons in the park pecking at popcorn. My mother fell asleep.

My father, alone now with his youngest son, began to tell me how terrible his children are for not calling or coming to visit. He called my oldest brother, whom I haven't seen in ten years, the lowest form of life on earth and referred to him as a disease, a blight. I listened to his monologue and wondered to myself if the insanity led to the drinking or if the drinking led to the insanity.

I asked for an alarm clock because I had to get up very early. They didn't have one. That made perfect sense to me. What would these people need a clock for? They aren't going anywhere.
I asked my father how I could get up in time and he said he would wake me. He told me that he only sleeps in one hour intervals with a half-hour wake time between each hour. I will believe anything in that house. I went to sleep with one eye open. I felt as if I were being watched. I wondered if his disease was in the air my child was breathing.

I woke up in a frenzy. I was running a little late and was in a full-fledged anxiety attack over the possibility that I might miss the bus and have to spend three more hours with my parents. It was 4:30 in the morning and my father had a pirate movie on the television. Some guy was getting run through with a sword and people were getting blown away by cannons and children were crushed by a collapsed mast and it was, I repeat, 4:30 on Sunday morning.

As soon as my father saw that I was upset and nervous, he began to talk about the futility of nervousness. He played on my discomfort. He, who had wrecked his life with neuroses and had been on Thorazine and vodka for fifty years trying to calm down, was making fun of me for being nervous. He said things like, "Dwight, you know you never could calm down." He knew I was dying to get away from him and he resented it.

He intentionally drove slowly through the empty, early morning streets. His routine was very familiar to me. It is a game called, "You are the Crazy One, I am Undaunted." While he was driving, he began to tell me a story about how some black man had recently given a speech in town and nearly caused a riot. He began to talk about violent confrontations and I said to him, "You're scaring my daughter." He shut up with resentment. Finally I had stood up to my father. It was in response to verbal violence in front of my daughter. I am not quite ready to stand up to him on my own behalf, but I am getting closer.

I wanted to lighten the conversation. "She's a wonderful girl, isn't she?" I said to my father. "So far," he replied. I went limp. That two-word answer summed up the way he always related to his own children. He negated them. His answer implied a belief that Celeste would grow up to be "no good." It also insinuated that no matter how wonderful she is, and no matter how well I am parenting her—it will have little or no effect on her worthiness as an adult. His statement was an insult to Celeste. It was a filthy thing to say. It was also an insult to me, as if to say: "Yeah, she is a good kid, but don't pat yourself on the back too soon. You were a good kid too and look what happened to you." He absolved himself of the tortures he inflicted on his children by saying that no matter what you do as a parent, the child might or might not grow up to be a loser. He seemed to be saying Celeste was a good child only because she was five years old and the quality of parenting had nothing to do with the emotional development. I can see why he would want to think that, considering how troubled all his children are.

There was a greater reason why I took Celeste to meet her grandparents for the first and, most likely, the last time. I wanted my father to validate me. My message to him was, "I am a good son and a good father. My daughter is a good child. Please love me." I was so very hungry for his love. I arrived hungry and I left hungry. I was asking of him something he was incapable of giving. It hurt. Not that I didn't see it coming. Not that I shouldn't have known better. It was a situation right out of the textbook. It was not that he was withholding love. It was that he didn't have it to offer.

Maybe it was hard for him to see his son being such a good father, knowing that he himself was such a bad one. Or perhaps he was silently cynical about me, just as he is cynical about everything else. Maybe he still considers himself to have been a good father cursed with lousy children. I guess I will never know why he could not or would not love me.

He said good-bye to us at the bus depot. It was as if he was saying good-bye to a store clerk after buying a package of cigarettes. His voice was as hollow as his soul. I couldn't detect an emotion in him from the moment we arrived to the moment we left. I went to meet my father and I met a shell of a man.

Celeste and I boarded the bus in the early morning darkness and headed for Disney World. I yearned for Mickey and Minnie and Pluto and Goofy. I yearned for contact with some lifeforms after our night in hell. I looked down at my daughter sleeping on my lap. I said a prayer of thanks that I survived that madhouse of my youth. And I said a prayer of thanks that the closest Celeste would ever get to a childhood like that would be to read these pages.

For a few minutes I tried to get angry at my parents. I tried to work up a good head of steam. I wanted to wear my anger like a suit of armor to spare me from the pain. But I couldn't. I never had a childhood and now I was losing my anger about never having had a childhood. What I was left with was...sadness.

I feel sorry for my parents. They have no relationship to speak of with their children. Now the same is true for their grandchildren. By trying to avoid the pain of life, they also avoided the joy. There is nothing I can do to change them. Once again I find myself powerless to save someone I love. They have a right to their own lives, no matter how tragic I consider them to be.

I really wish I had a gold thread I could sew around the border of this story. I wish I could crawl back into my fantasy bubble and report a happy ending. But that is not my story. A reconciliation seems more remote than ever. I must reject the naive notion that because I get better the world automatically follows suit.

My parents have led long and difficult lives. My life of hell ended when I entered recovery at the age of twenty-nine. My parents are a standard against which I can measure my growth. I have come a long, long way to where I am today. They are in their seventies and quite ill. The gamut of their emotional lives seems to only go between pain and numbness. They are not evil people. They are sad and troubled people, doing the best they can with the limited tools of living they have in their possession. I want to rewrite their lives. I want to open my chest and hand them my heart. I am strong. My heart can beat for the three of us. Here I am slipping back into my fantasy world again.

I can only save myself. I can build a life worth living to the best of my ability. I can look to my parents and learn from their mistakes. I can be grateful that I can look at the pitfalls they encountered and avoid some of them for myself. I am very sorry that, for reasons I will probably never know, my parents never found recovery. But I did. I have been spared. And my daughter is blessed with a sober father.

And, with his blessing and with this knowledge and insight, I will share my recovery with anyone who wants it. Recovery is contagious. I want to pass it along to whoever crosses my path. A lot of my strength I got from my parents. Many symptoms of the disease have been stripped away through hard work and the blessings of my Higher Power. I do not regret my past. I am not ashamed of it. My name is Dwight Lee Wolter and I am a proud man. I am the son of my father. We share the same blood. My family tree is blossoming after a long drought. A celebration is going on in my soul. Won't you join me?

I AM LOYAL TO MY DISEASE

I dreamed last night that my daughter was dead. I was crying and crying and while I was crying I spoke to her: "I will cry every Sunday for you. I will cry every Sunday for you forever." I woke up shaking. I told myself I could never survive the loss of my daughter. As I sat in my puddle of gloom and had my morning coffee, I began to think of the night before. What had I done or not done? What had I eaten or not eaten? What had I felt or refused to feel that would precipitate such a dream?

The night before I had been so lonely I sat catatonic on my chair. I'd sunk so low I could not move. I could not make a decision of where to go or what to do. I could not hold a thought. I felt as if I'd been involved in a bloodletting ritual that had gone a bit too far. I felt drained, empty, spiritually dead, unable to reach out or reach in. I felt like a tree in winter. I finally managed to move but it was only to walk toward the door and then turn around and go back to my chair. Then I would get up and walk toward the door and turn around and walk back to my chair again. Eventually I got out of the house and went to a calisthenics class at my health club. It shook me up a bit, but I still felt like dead meat. I went to a restaurant and had a cup of isolation soup and then I ate some dead meat. I force-fed myself because when I get depressed I starve myself. I have to put some weight on. I feel like a headache attached to a skeleton. I left the restaurant and went to one of the three self-help groups to which I belong. Several people were talking about the troubles they are having with their bosses.

I got up and walked out of the meeting and went to a meeting of one of my other self-help groups. The woman who was speaking was talking about picking losers for lovers. I identified with her all the way out the door. When I got outside I met up with some people I know. They invited me to go to have coffee at a restaurant with them and I agreed. I found myself quite attracted to one of the women in our group. I told her that she had lips exactly like Kim Basinger's. I told her that I was very attracted to Kim Basinger. She said Kim Basinger can't act. Then she said she wanted to be an actress. I smiled at her a lot and let her see me staring at her lips. We left the restaurant and walked up the street together. They were going to a party and invited me. The party, like the restaurant, was in the direction of my house. As a matter of fact, the party was around the corner from my house. I walked them to the party. We reached my apartment building, and just as they reached the door I turned away and said goodnight. They asked me again to come with them. I thanked them and walked away. I have been very upset with myself ever since.

I had been so very lonely. I remember telling myself that what I really hoped for was to run into a group of friends and be invited to a party. That is exactly what happened. And my response was to go home depressed and go to bed early so I could be well-rested for the nightmares and depression I woke up to. I had been with a woman I was attracted to, and my response was to walk away from her and wonder what it would have been like if I had stayed.

The scariest thing is that I don't know why I do this. I have been in recovery for six years. I have been in therapy for three years. I am intuitive. I am intelligent. And I don't know why I do this to myself. The closest I can get to the reason is a vague feeling that I am being loyal to someone or something. I seem to have a need and a desire to keep myself lonely and isolated. Who am I being loyal to by suffering like this? Am I doing penance for some horrible wrong I can't remember?

I am a very loyal person. I was loyal to my parents. I was loyal to my wife. I am loyal to my child. I am so loyal to my child that in my dream about her in which she died I declared that, as a statement of love and loyalty, I would cry every Sunday for her for the rest of my life. I have proved to myself and others time and again that I am a loyal person.

I am also loyal to my disease. My primary relationship has been to a diseased self for most of my life. I feel that I have been loyal to my disease because it stood by me for so long. For years I walked arm in arm down the street with my disease. We were the best of friends. We didn't need anyone else. We made perfect sense to each other.

But then the day came when I had to part with my disease if I wanted to survive. And my life has been much better since. But there are strongholds of resistance to recovery. I still, sometimes, follow the diseased dictates of my diseased thinking:

Thou Shalt Not Feel Free.

Thou Shalt Lead a Lonely Life.

The Sins of the Father Are Visited Upon the Son.

Thou Shalt Not Trust Friends.

I feel that if I give up my loyalty to my disease then I must give up my loyalty to my diseased parents. They taught me how to isolate myself. And to give up isolation is to give up what they had to offer. I remain true to my parents' values. And those values are currently extremely counterproductive to me. I suffer needlessly. This is not MY isolation. I learned it somewhere and am afraid to drop it.

But drop it I must. I have been loyal to my disease and now it is time to be loyal to my recovery. The rewards in store for me if I remain loyal to my disease are misery and early death. The best reward I can imagine would be a quasi-numbness, a life of no real pain but no real growth either. But the rewards I envision for loyalty to recovery, which is to say loyalty to myself, are immense. I don't want to die a lonely old man. I don't want to live as a lonely old man either. I want to connect with people. I want to be a part of the world. I want to be in love with a healthy person who loves me back. I want to have mutually respectful friendships. I want to have friendships with women that I don't feel the need to sexualize. I want some male buddies. I want to break out of my isolation cocoon, which keeps me warm but in which there is also no light. I want to break out of my loyalty to defeat.

I am sorry my parents lead desperately lonely, isolated lives. I cannot be like them and survive. By moving toward me, I am moving away from them. Most of what they taught me I have no use for. I must break the mold.

LET'S GET ON WITH IT

In order to forgive you, I must have already decided you are guilty of whatever I am about to forgive you for.

That means I have placed myself in the position of knowing who is guilty and who is not. Then I decide if you are to be punished or forgiven. I have adorned myself with a crown of resentments. I am the standard against which all goodness is measured. I am a self-appointed judge and executioner. I have relieved God of most of his duties.

I sit and wonder how I can forgive my parents without having judged them guilty. I can't. Guilty of what? Of having been ill? Of having been born into a bad family situation the same way I was?

I cannot forgive my parents if I cannot forgive myself. The executioner who screams, "Off with their heads!" every time I discover yet another way in which my parents couldn't properly nurture me is the same executioner who is out to get me every time I make a mistake. The executioner does not discriminate against me or others. The executioner wants blood. Any blood. The only way for me to be spared is to declare an unconditional amnesty for all prisoners of the disease. Then I and my parents and my friends and all the wounded, defensive people who suffer in silence and fear of retribution can come out and talk about what happened and where to go from here.

I am raising the white flag of enlightened surrender. Getting back, or getting over, or getting even is not the name of the game. The name of the game is LEARNING TO LOVE AND LIVE. Let's get on with it.

IT'S OFFICIAL

Today I came home and opened my mailbox to discover that I am divorced. I told myself I was going to organize a Divorce Party, but what I did instead was to go downtown to Soho and hang out alone in some art galleries, trying to hide from my feelings.

I have very mixed feelings about the divorce. I am trying to turn off my feelings like a drippy faucet right now, but I just said a prayer for the strength and courage and willingness and insight to persevere in the writing of this.

I fought very hard for the divorce. I have been separated for three long years. I have battled with my former wife for eighteen months, mostly over issues concerning our daughter. I won joint custody and totally equal rights with the mother concerning the welfare of the child. The battle cost me a fortune. I just got the final bill from my lawyer and I am dizzy with resentment. But I know it was worth every penny of it if it got me out of a bad marriage.

I left Soho and went to a meeting of a self-help group I joined two years ago to help me deal with the pain of separation. This self-help group concerns itself with relationships. It helps me to keep the focus on myself and not the other person. It helps me to examine the relationship but, most importantly, it stresses my role in it. I shared with the people there that two years ago I went to those rooms to find a way out of the pain. I discovered that those meetings would show me the way to become a more open, loving man. I admitted that I wanted to do that, not for my own benefit, but so that my estranged wife would want me back. It didn't work. She kept slipping farther and farther away from me and today is very much involved with another man. I became angry with the group, just as I became angry with my marriage counselor, just as I became angry at my God, for not saving my marriage. But I kept coming back and what I got instead was...

I saved me. I lost a marriage but I gained a self. I began to admit and accept, reluctantly, that the marriage was not worth saving, but I was. I realized that if a love like that came my way again I wouldn't take it. I might be tempted, since I am programmed to race toward unavailability, but I wouldn't hold on to it, at least for very long. That's improvement. That's increasing self-esteem.

So I lost the battle but I won the war. That marriage is kaput. I tried very, very hard to save the marriage. I tried very hard to reconcile with my former wife. I did my best and it was not good enough. This is sad. Dwight The Great bites the dust. But I have gone through changes that were essential to my becoming a whole person, which I could not have gone through had I remained in that marriage. One door closed and another door opened.

I feel good today. Bittersweet. Mostly sweet. I feel more like a man than I ever have before. I'm not even sure what that means but it feels good. I feel healthy and strong and good-looking. I feel talented and intelligent and hopeful. I feel that I am embarking on yet another new beginning, that my life has been worth living and the best is yet to come. I am narrowing the gap between me and my potential. I would have settled for so little two years ago. I would have settled for having my painful marriage back. But what I have been granted instead is far more than I would ever have known to ask for.

STOP!

I have been granted the power to stop
the cycle of abuser and abused.
It must begin somewhere.
Let it begin with me.
Though treating others with
respect and dignity
is foreign to me
and feels like betrayal
of my family tradition,
I will do it anyway.
The chain of bondage
is only as strong
as its weakest link.
I am the weakest link.
I quit the chain gang.
My family might not recognize me
anymore. But I will recognize me
as a leader in my family's
new generation of freedom.

A FUNNY THING HAPPENED TO ME ON THE WAY TO RECOVERY

I quit drinking. It is too dangerous. Then I quit drugs. Ditto. A while later I quit smoking cigarettes. Double ditto. Eventually I quit drinking soda and eating candy. Red meat became repulsive so I quit that too. I went to the dentist and the doctor. I began to ride a bicycle. I pedal my resentments away. Good way to work out anger. Then I began to see a chiropractor because of my lousy posture and lower back pains. He relieved the pain and got me on a program of stretch exercises.

I joined a couple of self-help groups, a single parents' group, and I started therapy. I began to keep a diary. Then I began to write this book.

I began to read spiritual literature first thing every morning and the last thing every night. I got a new address book and filled it with telephone numbers of people I respect and I began to use those numbers. I availed myself to people who asked for my help and friendship. I began to listen without judgment. I began to speak without editing each sentence before saying it. I began to take risks necessary to actualize my goals and dreams. I began to listen to suggestions without feeling that I had to do everything you said—or nothing you said. I learned how to hold a job for more than two months. I learned how to take orders from my boss without feeling like a slave.

I began to trust my instincts. I began to view time as an ally. I began to become process- rather than results-oriented. I began to perceive God as my trusted companion, rather than as a punitive dictator.

I began to see my parents as sick people, perhaps too sick to seek treatment. I began to see them as victims of their disease, rather than as instigators of my disease. I began to see people as people, not as two-dimensional stick figures to be moved around like stage props.

I began to see myself as a fragile yet potent spirit embodied in a temple of flesh which I must respect and carefully maintain. I began to view life as a precious moment in an eternity of being. I began to see my problems as opportunities to resolve the issues presented to me, rather than as hostile obstacles to overpower. I began to watch my life unfold, rather than trying to pry it open. I began to let experiences happen through me, rather than to collect them like butterflies in a scrapbook. I began to empty myself each day, in order to be filled anew. I began to feel free, and open, and willing to let new and better things come into my life. I began to expect goodness. I began to feel I deserved it. Then I began to receive it. I began to regret nothing. I began to see all my experiences as part of the process of recovery from a life of numbness and dread. I began to feel hope. I began to live a life of faith and action. I began to trust that I would be all right. I began to look forward to each day, even the difficult ones. I began to live. I began to realize my suffering was necessary in order for me to appreciate life as I know it today. My life has been spared at the point where many others have perished. For that I am eternally grateful.

MY 'X' IS GETTING MARRIED

I used to be afraid to go into Central Park on Saturdays. I feared that I would see my daughter, Celeste, riding on the shoulders of another man.

I feared the worst and it has happened. I got a letter the other day from my former wife stating that she is getting married. She asked for my "understanding." I told myself that I will offer her more than that. I will offer her my blessing. I wish the best for her and her new husband.

I hope this is the final level of letting go that I have to do. Whenever I think of what happened to our marriage and our family, a small part of me still screams, "Tell me it isn't true!" I wish I didn't have to admit to the unwelcome feeling summed up in that cliche about relationships past: even though I don't want her, I don't want anyone else to have her either. I truly have a double standard.

The bulk of the pain I feel is in relation to my daughter. On a conscious level, everything is fine. My daughter is seven. I have been a single parent with joint custody since she was two. She doesn't remember her parents having lived together. Sometimes, neither do I. All that remains of my marriage are a few photos and a hazy feeling like Novocain wearing off.

My daughter and I have a great relationship. I have been present for her to the best of my ability since the moment she was born. I did not abandon her when I divorced her mother—as many men often do, if not physically, then emotionally. I am as much a

Mommy as a Daddy. I am the breadwinner and the bread-baker. I am the head of the household and the house-husband. I am the nurturer and the discipliner. I know how to cuddle, cook, sew, braid hair, run a business, iron, and—yes—I even know how to carve a turkey.

All who have met me, without exception, know that I am a very good father. No one and nothing, except me, can change that. Then why, if I consider myself such a great father, do I take pen to paper to convince myself? Why do I have recurring dreams of tidal waves swooshing down and smashing everything I love to bits? Why, since I heard of the impending marriage, do I want to call my daughter every hour that she is with her mother to make sure our relationship is intact?

Somewhere deep inside me I am afraid I am going to lose the love of my daughter. Parenting is where I put most of my love, my energy, my hope. I have never allowed myself to love like this. I remember when I first separated from my wife, I immediately began to withdraw from my daughter. I could not separate loving her from loving her mother. She reminded me so much of her mother, I felt I had to detach from one in order to detach from the other. I feel fortunate that I saw this happening as soon as it began and was able to begin the long journey of accepting and nourishing my daughter as a completely autonomous person, even though she was only two years old.

But I still feel threatened. The thought of another man entering the picture makes me physically sick! I feel weak and pale. I wish there was an express elevator to carry the blood back into my face.

I told myself, after reading the letter, that parenting is very difficult and maybe the presence of a stepfather could allow me to take a step back from my immense responsibilities and focus on my writing a bit more. The stepfather could take over for a while. What I was experiencing was a fear-driven rationalization to withdraw from love. I was trying to be so cool. But I was really terrified.

"Don't call him Daddy! Don't be with him more than you are with me!! Please don't take my baby!!!" Those were the thoughts and feelings that flooded me. "That's what you get for loving," the nasty voice of a sick conscience told me. For so long in my life the price of love was loss. I didn't dare to care because I felt the source of my affections would either leave me or be taken away. And, as much as I wanted to resist it, this "step-bastard" walking into my life triggered all these ancient feelings.

I fear that I am being replaced. I am tempted to resort to my old way of dealing with these feelings, which is to run away. But I can't. I feel stuck with my feelings like something awful on the bottom of my shoe. Panic! I can't get the shoe off! Will these horrible feelings ever fade?

I decided to stop fighting the raging thoughts and let the feelings enter. I can control my thoughts—but I cannot control my feelings. Like a flu, these painful feelings will run their course. I will endure the fever and then watch it pass.

I feel the urge to compete with my X and her soon-to-be husband. (I love calling her my X—that X on the page seems to sum up our relationship so perfectly.) I hate to compete. I was the youngest child in my family and competing with my siblings seemed futile. As a young adult, I would refuse to compete with other men for the affections of a woman. As soon as another interested man entered the scene, I would drop out. I was terrified of rejection. To compensate for this fear, the pendulum swung in the other direction. I would tend to annihilate the competition. From job-seeking to the most informal games of sports—my style could best be called "overkill." Both extremes of my reaction to competition point to my utter terror of abandonment.

I found myself acting in a one-sided competition. I had to be the first person to take my daughter to see the Christmas windows at Macy's and to the *Nutcracker* ballet at Lincoln Center. I am famous for my Easter egg hunts and for ringside seats at the Big Apple Circus. Nothing but the best for Celeste. Why? Mostly for her, but partially for me. Mostly out of love, but partially out of fear. I feel I must prove myself to Celeste, like I am auditioning for the coveted role of being her permanent father.

I remind myself that these feelings are mine, not hers. She would be happy taking an apple and a friend to the playground. It is I who feels that I must measure the love of my daughter against the price of a circus ticket.

Celeste loves me unconditionally. I am the one who sees limits to her ability to love me. I am the one who fears that I can be replaced by any man with a smile, a candy bar, and knowledge of how to get to the Carousel by way of the hot dog stand.

It makes me sad that, as a parent, my self-esteem is sometimes still low. It makes me sad that I don't have a family to offer to myself and to my daughter. I am a firm believer that it takes three or more to make a family. I don't know what it feels like to turn to a sibling, parent, or spouse and discuss what is going on in our lives. I long for this. I am tired of being a Bachelor Father Living in New York.

I am jealous of my X and her new beau. My X is from a family that gives parties in Chicago, goes on vacations in Paris, and has picnics in Cape Cod with lots of children running around. The children gather around the holiday tree in their pajamas and, as they open presents, the adults bring out pictures from the season before to comment on how much they have grown and changed. There are feasts in the country home of a family member at Thanksgiving. I allow my daughter to go to all these events, rather than to spend the holiday alone with me, because I want her to be happy and have the experience of family.

I notice as I write this that I speak of these feelings of a healthy family as if they will never be within reach. I long for, rather than hope for, a healthy family. Although it is true that I have never had a sense of family, I must complete the sentence by saying that I have never had a sense of family YET.

I am in the final stages of letting go of my X. I am also letting go of my daughter, and trying to accept that she will be, in part, parented by a man I do not know. Damn! It was painful to write those last two sentences. The reality settles in. And it hurts. But as I process this new awareness, I hope that the sediment—the soil—at the bottom of this experience is love.

As the pain lifts, and a broader perspective returns, I realize that not all of me hurts. And the part of me that does hurt will not hurt forever.

Pain is indeed a great teacher. Because of my personal growth during my divorce, I have avoided choosing another inappropriate partner. I have also been able to build a family of choice to supplement my spiritual needs, which were not met by my family of origin. I am developing a close network of friends from a fellowship I belong to, from meetings I attend, from work, and from my health club. My daughter has the opportunity to do the same. It is great that we are both learning that you don't have to—and indeed can't—get all your needs met by one person.

Celeste wants to be happy. Celeste wants her mother and father to be happy also. Celeste deserves to love someone without fearing that by loving him she is being disloyal to me. I do not want to teach my daughter how to withhold love. The man my X is marrying is a good person. He is and always has been good to Celeste. My daughter is very lucky. She has the strong support of many people who love her.

I want to be happy. I want to live in a large, well-rounded world. I want to be free to love. I want to encourage love in all its manifestations.

I remember all too well the tremendous pain I experienced in releasing my wife. I remember waking up in the middle of the night after a nightmare about my wife being with another man. I was sweating and panting and felt like a lung had been torn out of me in my sleep and now I couldn't breathe without her.

Today I see my former wife as a separate, autonomous person who is trying, like me, to lead a healthy life and to raise a healthy child. Times have changed. I have changed. For the better. Celeste is free to ride on the shoulders of her stepfather anytime she likes. There is enough love to go around.

I SEE I SEE

I see big changes in little things:

The way I listen with an open mind.
The way I strike up conversations with
people on the bus when I used to be
withdrawn and silent. The way I offer
friendship without seeking reward.
The way I keep my day full and
interesting. The way I am less afraid
to be alone. The way I am less afraid
to be with people. The way I am less
afraid to be with God.

I see God in little things:

A pigeon feather zigzagging its way
down from the rafters of a cathedral.
My daughter saying her prayers. An old
couple eating hot dogs on a park bench.
A pregnant woman studying her reflection
in a shop window with a pleased look
on her face.

To see the world with childlike wonder
is a great gift. But it is also a craft,
honed from the willingness to see the world
as you know it disappear each night
only to be rebuilt each day with patient
hands, a loving heart, and a faith
that binds the hands and the heart
together.

I see God in me:

I pray for courage
to keep my fist unclenched, palm facing
upward in a symbol of openness and
readiness to receive the goodness
I have worked so hard for
and finally believe I deserve.

AS I SEE IT NOW

The chaos was not my fault. Craziness is not a moral issue. Disease is not a moral issue. It is a physical, mental, and spiritual issue, but not a moral one. So I do not blame myself for what happened in my crazy life, nor do I accept blame that others try to put on me. It is hard to accept when things go as wrong as they did in my life that there are no villains, only victims.

A plague, like alcoholism, will snake its way through a population, leaving in its wake a mass of people wandering around sick and tired and confused and, as if that isn't bad enough, they strain their brains trying to figure out what they did wrong to deserve such a fate.

"I DID NOTHING WRONG! WHY ME?" I shouted heavenward.

"WHY NOT YOU?" I heard shouted back so quick I thought at first it was an echo. Perhaps I was hit and hit hard by this plague because my Higher Power knew that I was strong enough to take it, and to live through it, and to talk about it to you, and to my nephew, and to my daughter, and eventually to my parents.

Acceptance is weird. I have learned that I have a disease. I have learned that no matter what I do I cannot change the way I was brought up. I have learned that I am stuck with this disease; I will never shake it. After a lifetime of fighting, I have learned the war is over and I lost. My job now is to accept myself for who I am and where I came from. It is so bizarre that it is through the acceptance, not the fighting or the anger or the repulsion, that the change comes. As I begin to let go of my past, I learn to embrace my future.

If the chaos, the craziness, the disease was not my fault, then it wasn't my parents' fault either. Damn! Here I am left with no one to blame again. You mean my former wife is just another struggling person with problems of her own and I can't blame her either? You mean everyone is at least a little bit crazy and everyone has hurt someone and gotten hurt in the process? You mean that if I want to learn to forgive myself I have to learn to forgive my parents? What a trap! I wanted to get off easy—point a finger at someone and walk away in disgust and self-righteous indignation. You mean if I point the finger at anyone, I am perpetuating the problem? Why?

Acting out the symptoms of the disease has got to stop somewhere. My parents were brought up the same way I was. They taught what they knew. They were not parented well, so where were they to get the information to learn to parent well? Go to a meeting? Join a club? Read a book? Hire an enlightened shrink? My parents weren't as lucky as I have been.

My recovery is a fight. It has been GRANTED to me. I did not earn it or buy it or steal it or get it through correspondence school. The heavens conspired to save me. My father is so much stronger than me in many ways, yet I am the one who has broken out of the web of addiction. The shy little crippled boy turned out to be amazingly strong. There was no indication in my life that this would happen. My life being spared was a gift, not an acquisition. I am a lucky one.

You, reading this book, are a lucky one too. Two close friends have relapsed into their disease since I began writing this book. One of them was my sponsor in a recovery group. I have been around the block at least twice unescorted, but in all my worldly wisdom I would never have guessed that either of these people would have picked up a glass of death and put it to their lips.

I am a man with troubles. I live day to day with a disease in remission. I am sometimes confused and weary. I feel, whether it is true or not, that I have to work harder at life than most people do. But having been through what I have been through has sharpened my vision. Out of the chaos, my parents crafted a strong and talented man.

I carry my recovery like a precious gift that God has placed in my hand, knowing that if I drop it, it will break. I work hard to keep it clean and polished. It took every single day of my life to get me to this moment. Without the tragedy I have suffered, I would not have been motivated to get to know myself as well as I have. I might have died a stranger unto myself. I might have died before I lived. How ironic—that partly because I felt bad in the past I feel good today.

I have looked back but I did not stare. There is no future there. Looking back has not killed me as I once feared it would. My past did not swallow me up like a huge wave that would tumble me to pieces. No, looking back did not kill me, but it did not save me either. Looking back has given me insight into the solution, but is not the solution itself.

I am not responsible for the plague that struck me and my family. But having visited the damage, I feel responsible to myself to pull myself up from the wreckage, dust myself off, clean my wounds, and get on with the rest of my life. Because I survived the alcoholocaust I feel responsible to help others to do the same. I want to pass on the legacy of help and love that was so freely handed to me by fellow troubled souls in the three recovery groups to which I belong. I no longer fear responsibility the way I once did. I embrace it as an opportunity to grow closer to the person I want to become.

Writing this book has helped me immensely. I hope that when my daughter grows up and reads this book, it will spare her some needless suffering. I hope this book has helped you. Thanks for being there for me.

I WONDER

I wonder if earth
is the womb of God
and we are all
just walking around
waiting to be born?

ABOUT THE AUTHOR

Dwight Lee Wolter lives in New York City with his daughter, Celeste. He is a poet, journalist, and performance artist, with a special interest in the issues of single parents, and of adults who grew up in families affected by alcoholism and other dysfunctions. In Wisconsin he was a member of the Governor's Council on Children and Youth, a member of the Poetry in the Schools program, and a state champion original orator. He is co-founder of Quest Publishing, and editor and publisher of Nobody Press.

He is also the author of another 1989 book, *Forgiving Our Parents* (CompCare Publishers), for adult children from dysfunctional families.